Warring For My Girls

We **Pray** Together, We **Slay** Together

A 30-Day Devotional for Friends

By Mya K. Douglas

Dedication:

This book is dedicated to my lifetime bestie, my mother, Linda M. Douglas. I love you endlessly.

To my childhood bestie, Erica L. Bailey-Paul – thank you for everything.

And to Jesus Christ – the greatest friend a girl will ever have. Thank you for loving me back together.

To women everywhere: When we heal, the world heals. Get your healing, sis. Get your healing.

Table of Contents

5

Introduction

Friendships. It's one of the hardest relationships to navigate. I spent many seasons alone trying to understand the true meaning of friendship. This could only be done by studying my relationship with Jesus Christ. Friendships are a beautiful translation of God's love for us expressed through the individuals that He places in our lives. Did you catch that? *That He places in our lives.* If we dismiss God's provision of friendships by choosing what fulfills our own selfish desires and not His unique plan for our lives as it pertains to these relationships, we can never excel in this area.

Women across the world are struggling in their friendships, and after a certain age, the idea of maintaining fruitful, equally balanced friendships, seems far-fetched. Add to the mix social media (and at the time this book is being written, social distancing), and you've got a social tug of war going on. We're all trying to develop a solid connection with people while enduring the complications of technical difficulties and misunderstandings of the heart's expressions.

I chose to write this prayer devotional for two reasons: One, God told me to. It wasn't even on my agenda; and two, I've experienced a beautiful, lifelong friendship for more than thirty years. Between the divine wisdom of God, coupled with the many ups and downs I've experienced in many of my friendships, my expertise is clear – *I learned to become the friend I desired to have.* Much of what I'm sharing with you here is exactly what I've walked through to become the sister-friend I needed and to identify the kind of sister-friends I know God wants me to have.

My prayer is that as God leads you to the women of God who are assigned to your life, both seasonally and lifetime, you will experience the following:

1) That you will become more of the sister-friend you desire, *and...*
2) You will draw closer to Christ so that He can transform your friendships into what He desires.

Lastly, I love you, sis. Not because I know you, but because you're opting to challenge yourself in this area and – that *ain't* easy. I admire you for taking the leap. Trust me. You won't regret it.

Love, Mya Kay.

War 1 - Warring for Christ-Centered Friendships

Dear Heavenly Father,

Before I cover anything, I pray that You would send me Christ-centered friendships. This doesn't mean I have to throw away those who You've placed around me, but it does mean if they start to fall away after this prayer, I need to understand that who You pick for me is greater than anyone I could ever pick for myself. I pray that I continue to grow my walk with You and that I let nothing stand in the way of that. I pray that the God-fearing women You send me are also investing heavily in their relationship with Christ. I thank You in advance for the wisdom I will learn from these women and I pray that You teach me how to be a source of wisdom for them. I pray for these new friendships, asking that You help me recognize anyone the enemy may send in place of what I really need. I cancel the assignment of the enemy over my Godly, ordained friendships. I pray for us to see each other the way You see us, to value what You've placed inside of us, and to honor each other vastly. I thank You in advance that I will receive who You send, even if it's not someone I expected or someone I think I need. I trust You with the decision to choose my friends for me. In Jesus' name, Amen.

Anchor Verse: Amos 3:3 (NKJV)

Can two walk together, unless they are agreed?

Scriptures to meditate on: **Ecclesiastes 4:9-10, 1 Corinthians 15:33, Proverbs 22:24-25**

War 2 - Warring for Her Relationship with Christ

Dear Heavenly Father,

One of the things I've always valued about my friend is that we both know You. We have a solid relationship that rests solely on You. However, I know that we can't get complacent in our walk. I pray that my sister is seeking Your face daily – before watching *The Breakfast Club*, listening to *The Steve Harvey Morning Show*, or listening to her playlists. I pray that she understands keeping You first means sacrificing many of the things that have become her norm. The things that she used to find comfort in, I pray that she finds comfort in You. Things that she uses to fill a void, I pray that she would allow You to fill that void. I pray that when she seeks Your word and sits at Your feet in the morning, that she would truly surrender her will and pick up Yours. I pray that she is fully invested in the relationship she has with You, even more than she is invested in ours. I pray that You would speak clearly to her and reveal how You speak to her so that she never misses Your voice. Lead her to the rock that is higher than her. Lead her to a higher place in You in every season. I pray healing over her mind so that she can clearly hear Your thoughts. Continue to help her develop the fruits of the spirit, even if that means being in uncomfortable situations and circumstances that force her to grow. If she comes to me seeking wisdom and advice, I pray that You help me not to speak until you give me the words to say. Help me always speak the truth in love and not hold back out of fear. I pray that she would find herself in Your word daily. Lead her to passages that speak directly to her situation and her heart. I pray that the word would always fall on fertile ground and that she will continue to water that seed until she grows in that area. Anyone or anything that keeps her from getting closer to You, remove it now. Deliver her from it and give her a smooth transition as she surrenders fully to You. Lastly, may she continue to cultivate her relationship with you more than any other relationship in her life. Show her what that looks like. In Jesus' name, Amen.

The Breakdown

Your friend's relationship with Christ is the most valuable, unbreakable, and stable relationship she will ever build upon – even more than the one she has with you, and it should be. We often negate praying for our friends' relationship with Christ with the same fervor as the way we pray for our relationship with them. Naturally, our flesh is selfish. We want our relationships to thrive, along with our jobs, our finances, our children, our careers, and everything about us.

But what if you prayed that Christ would stretch her faith and pull her closer into Him, even if that meant she would go through a season or two without you guys being in touch? Where your "stuck-like-glue" foundation was shaken to its core so that God could do the work in her *and* you that

He needs to? Your prayers should be that His will for the relationship will manifest. Far too often, women jump headfirst into most, if not *all*, relationships.

You have to keep Christ at the center of your friendship and ask God regularly if this friendship is fulfilling the purpose that He intended. In my opinion, it appears like having Godly friends is undervalued in our society. I think people post that they want praying friends, and they may even portray the image of wanting to be Godly – but following Christ requires a real dedication to the things of God. With that said, most people want God but don't really want "the Christian walk". They want just enough of Him to experience Heaven, but not all of the growth and sacrifice in between. I have this saying, "for many people, it's easier to stay in bondage because it's comfortable." Getting free and staying free requires work, sacrifice, and discipline.

> *You have to keep Christ at the center of your friendship and ask God regularly if this friendship is fulfilling the purpose that He intended.*

Commercial Break: I'm a firm believer that we should, as required by God, love everyone. Walking in love is the way we show God's love. But as a believer, woman of God, and prayer warrior, your closest friends should be believers as well. The Word clearly says, "how can two walk together unless they agree." People hurriedly apply that to marriage, but this applies to any "two" people. My closest friends have to be able to cover me in prayer, encourage and lift me up with God's wisdom (not the world's or even her own philosophies) and hold me accountable based on His word. I'm not saying that someone of another faith or someone who doesn't believe can't give valuable advice or doesn't have wisdom; it's the source of that wisdom and advice that concerns me. Be wise in who you're connected to. Now, back to our regularly scheduled program.

With that, I want to answer a question many people have. Should a fruitful, Christian woman befriend women who aren't Christians? Clear and cut answer: No. Christ loved everyone but only chose the select few who were willing to lay down their lives to follow Him. Many people that we cross paths with, and that God aligns us with, are assignments – we're the ones who turn them into friendships.

The other piece to this is that many women enter friendships and then pray *after* they start experiencing betrayals, heartbreaks, and frustrations in that friendship. If we would seek God's will first, instead of going to Him to fix the crisis, we would avoid a lot of turmoil. Ask yourself this question. Are any of my friendships surface level? Or are they really rooted in Christ? My advice would be to study Ruth and Naomi's friendship (the book of Ruth in the bible), so you can better understand the dynamics of a powerful, Godly friendship. In season one, episode four of my Podcast, *The Girl Files,* there's an episode called "Failed Friendships" where I speak on this.

As I close this chapter out, I want to propose another question. Why do we pray and fast for our future spouse but somehow don't apply those same principles to finding and developing friendships with women? Think about it. If you have solid, Godly friendships, keep praying, and warring for your sister-friend because the enemy hates unions. Prayers are our first line of defense.

Anchor Verse: John 15:4 (TPT = The Passion Translation)
So you must remain in life-union with me, for I remain in life-union with you. For as a branch severed from the vine will not

bear fruit, so your life will be fruitless unless you live your life intimately joined to mine.

Scriptures to meditate on: **John 15 (whole chapter)**

War 3 - Warring for Her When Her Womb is Filled (Spiritually)

Dear Heavenly Father,

L ord, I come before You with this new idea/concept/project that my sister is trying to birth. I thank You for giving her the vision to see past this moment to bring forth what You've trusted her with. I pray that she uses wisdom when sharing this idea with anyone that You haven't given her permission to. I pray that she doesn't spoil the blessing by speaking too soon. I pray that wisdom would fall on her right now. Bless her creativity, give her insight, and increase her capacity to bring forth this idea the way You see it. I come against the enemy that would try to cause her to miscarry by going into premature labor by rushing ahead of You. I pray that she works diligently on what You've given her and that she doesn't try to move ahead of You by putting the cart before the horse. It's easy to allow the excitement to cause us to move too fast, but You have a set date that You want her to launch and release what You've given her. I ask that whatever that date is, that she would write the vision, make it plain and stick with that date. I pray that no matter what tries to hinder the release or what comes against her, that she will trust that You can see further than her. I pray against the spirit of frustration that would try to keep her from moving forward in faith. I bind every negative principality that would try to whisper in her ear that she "can't" do what You've called her to do. Reveal to her the resources You've blessed her with to bring this "baby" to term. You know the oil she carries, so I pray that You help her see herself beyond this moment. Give her a glimpse of the end so she can see what she's reaching for. If she's going in a direction that You don't want her to go in, I ask that You redirect her right now. God, bless this idea with favor and bring the right connections and people into her space who can help her birth what she's carrying. Give me the understanding and wisdom I need to be supportive. If there's something I can do to help her, reveal it to me. If not, help me to continue to pray for her and step aside so that she can grow into this moment. I pray that she'll only be surrounded by people who can help run with her and not those who want to compete with her. Thank You for this blessing that will be a blessing to the nations. In Jesus' name, Amen.

The Breakdown

Birthing an idea into today's world is scary. You contend with the emotions that try to overpower you daily. Emotions and thoughts that run wild make you think that you won't be able to really get out what's down on the inside of you. I can be honest and say that most of what I've worked on in the past, I didn't share with my friends during the stages where I was building. I grew up in North Philadelphia, and much of what I've done, I didn't always have a solid blueprint for. I had to find women that were in the space I was currently creating in. That wasn't always easy.

On most days, I had to fight against my own mediocrity and tell myself that I could do it, even when nobody else was around to encourage me. Women desire to have someone rooting for them. I don't care if you're Oprah, Michelle Obama, or Meg Thee Stallion – we want someone that's going to root for us. My childhood bestie was always super supportive, even if she didn't fully understand what I was working on. Support goes a long way because days will come where you'll question your own abilities.

The key is to understand that having a friend war for you in this area is priceless. You're going to endure some pretty big challenges along this bumpy road, and similar to natural pregnancy, there will be times you'll be worn out and can't even see your next step – but God can. And that friend warring for you will make sure you can, too. One of the things I had to humble myself and learn is this: Just because I was praying for her business, project, or new idea didn't mean I was privy to what she was working on. Ouch!

Most of us feel like our friends *owe* us access to *every* part of their life, especially if it was that way in previous seasons. Maybe they did tell you all of their secrets and you could always count on her for the "tea" (we'll be praying about gossip in another chapter), but you have to be willing to pray this prayer even if you don't know the details. If you truly have your friend's best interest at heart and not your own selfish desires, you can war for her without the need to be standing right next to her on the battlefield.

> *If you truly have your friend's best interest at heart and not your own selfish desires, you can war for her without the need to be standing right next to her on the battlefield.*

Anchor Verse: Proverbs 24:3 (TPT)

Wise people are builders – they build families, businesses, communities. And through intelligence and insight, their enterprises are established and endure.

Scriptures to meditate on: **Isaiah 66:9**

War 4 - Warring for Her When Her Womb is Filled (Naturally)

Dear Heavenly Father,

My sister is carrying a new life inside her womb, and she's excited. I'm thankful that You would fill her womb at this time. She and her husband have been waiting and longing for this moment, and this is a special time for them. I'm praying that You would cover this pregnancy with Your spirit, power, and strength. On the days when she feels tired, be her supernatural strength. I pray for a protective barrier to cover this baby and ask that You would cancel the assignment of the enemy that would try to bring destruction or death to her womb. I cancel the assignments of miscarriage, high-risk pregnancy symptoms, and stress. I pray peace, increase, favor, and blessing over her womb. Give her wisdom on foods to eat that will aid in having a healthy pregnancy. Honor her cravings and give her a boost of confidence when she looks in the mirror and sees more than she desires (wink). I pray that on the days she's tired, You give her husband strength to cover the baby in prayer and to war for their child. Give them both insight into who this child is early on, so they know the prayers to pray and the war to wage against the enemy's camp. I pray wisdom over her and that she would listen to the advice of strong mothers who have gone before her and even her husband when he tells her to rest and take it easy. I ask that when unbearable pain hits, that You comfort her immediately. Give her instinct and unction to know when to seek her doctor's wisdom. I come against the spirit of stubbornness and pray that You would increase her desire to lean into You more. I pray over her endeavors, her business, and any projects that she may have started before she learned that she was pregnant.

Help her not to hurry back to the norm, but to accept this as part of her new norm and trust You with those things that she's already built. You know what she needs, and You know what her projects and businesses need, so give her rest in her heart to trust her team, partners, and anyone that You've sent to help her in this season. I pray over her womb and ask that You increase her joy whenever she feels the baby kicking. I pray a supernatural barrier over her amniotic sac and decree she will carry this baby to term and have a happy, healthy, and blessed baby. In Jesus' name, Amen.

The Breakdown

Years ago, one of my friends found out she was pregnant. By this time, she had been dealing with diabetes for a while. During her pregnancy, there was always a concern that her sugar would drop, which of course, left doctors concerned about the baby. One time, while I was working overnight, she texted me from the hospital because she was super stressed. She was clearly scared because she had *never seen this moment before.* As I covered her in prayer, I felt the uneasiness in her voice melting away.

Commercial Break: I emphasized "never seen this moment before" because I know we often miss the moments

God is stretching us to be more selfless than we've ever been. When we realize that most of what our friends go through is new, we can understand the need to have more grace. Now, back to our regularly scheduled program.

When I was pregnant at nineteen, my childhood bestie called me right when I was having a depressing moment. I was sitting at my dining room table while working on some college coursework. I was so down that I couldn't even eat. When I answered the phone, I was honest with her. I was depressed and hurting. I felt like I'd let myself and everyone else down. That phone call meant so much to me. She was encouraging, and I knew God had sent her to be the light in that dark moment. Ultimately, I would lose the baby due to an ectopic pregnancy.

The flip side to this is that some women may find out their friend is pregnant while they're waiting to conceive. Many wives go through this, and it can be hard to keep praying for your friend when you're waiting for your moment. Just keep in mind that Elizabeth (from the Bible) waited a very long time, and once she did get pregnant, she was beyond joyful. However, let's use a modern-day example so we can see how powerful God's timing is.

Remember when Remy Ma and Papoose became pregnant (for those who don't know, they are both rappers)? I know you probably watched that episode of *Love & Hip Hop*, so don't lie (I'm laughing). She experienced an ectopic pregnancy and ended up losing the baby. After several more attempts, they ended up having a beautiful baby girl. Can you imagine waiting years to be reunited with your husband, building your budding family, finally getting pregnant, and then losing the baby you've been praying and waiting for? That was their story.

Days turn into weeks, and weeks turn into years, but it doesn't mean that God is ignoring you. He knows what your body can handle and *when* it can handle the weight of a baby; He knows how stable you and your husband need to be in your finances so that you'll be able to support the blessing you're praying for. He also knows the timing of the doors that will open around you. In other words, that business you prayed for *first* might be getting ready to take off and God doesn't want you to bring a baby into the world that you may not have the capacity to nurture the way He sees fit. But God does have a way of lining things up so that what normally would be hard and unbearable is covered under a grace and peace that you won't be able to explain.

> *God does have a way of lining things up so that what normally would be hard and unbearable is covered under a grace and peace that you won't be able to explain.*

Does that mean that life will always be perfect, and God is waiting for perfection before He blesses your womb to carry life? No. Life happens. Even in the best of circumstances, you'll still need to pray and wage war when the enemy roars his ugly head. That's why it pays to wait for *your* season.

Anchor Verse: Psalm 127:3 (TPT)

Children are God's love-gift; they are heaven's generous reward.

Scriptures to meditate on: **Psalm 139:13-18, 1 Samuel 1**

War 5 - Warring for Her During Seasons of Disconnect

Dear Heavenly Father,

Can we talk? Okay. So, the truth is, I feel a bit lost. I know that my sister is doing her thing and that You have moved her into a new season of life, but I would be lying if I said I didn't feel left out. As time has gone on, I realize that we aren't connecting like we used to, and it seems that busyness has gotten in the way of our relationship. I am thankful and grateful that You would bless her and cause her to grow, but I'm asking for peace and understanding. I bind the spirit of jealousy, confusion, and the taunting that the enemy is trying to convey to my heart. I know that this season is meant for me to cultivate and grow what You've placed in my heart, so help me to redirect my heart in that area. God, give me the grace and balance to still be a good friend and check on my sister, even when she isn't checking on me. This is new for her. She's never seen this season before, and neither have I. Therefore, I'm asking that You speak to her heart. Continue to increase her wisdom, knowledge, and understanding in this season. Help her to follow Your leading and guidance. Help me know that if You don't have us hanging out or talking as much, it's not to hurt us or make either of us feel slighted or alone. It's for the benefit of us growing closer to You and coming out of this season better than when we entered it. I pray that if You have her in a space where You want her focused on You and her goals, that she let nothing distract her. I pray that she would have a spirit of discernment like never before. I pray that the fear of the Lord rests on her so that she would make wise decisions that honor You. Now, God, I ask that You heal my heart. It's not easy dealing with this type of change. I know that it would be easier to lie and say it doesn't hurt, but I'm grateful to serve a God that wants me to come to Him in truth – because You already know how I'm feeling. You love when I come to you bearing all because that means I trust You with ALL, and all areas of my life need Your covering, Your love, and Your touch. Give me the strength to do what You say, no matter how I feel. In Jesus' name, Amen.

The Breakdown

We've all been here before. Literally walked through a moment where we know that we prayed for our friend to have much success and that blessings would chase her down wherever she goes, but many of us didn't think that would mean we might not get to share in those blessings with her. I'm betting many of us even felt the strain of jealousy trying to cause us to send a text that went something like this: "Hey sis. Listen, I know you're working hard, and I'm proud of you, but I really feel like you're changing. I'm happy for you, but I was there for you when you needed the prayers for this new business you started, and now, I feel like you've just totally forgotten me. I'm not asking you to slow down, but what's up?"

That was the sweet, perhaps Southern Belle version. My version would've been laced with a bit more fire than that. I had to rebuke the spirit of North Philly as I was typing this. I know you're probably chuckling, but it's true. There have been so many times in my past where I literally had to hit delete and put my phone down because I couldn't understand nor fathom how it made sense that *I* wouldn't be a part of any season of a friend's life. I mean, we're supposed to be friends, *right?* Well, here's what God revealed to me throughout my friendships over the years:

1) God controls the seasons and who we have in each one. Every season carries an assignment, and no matter how much we love and value someone, if that season isn't supposed to include them, it just won't. If you feel excluded, know that God is intentional. Pass the test so that when your season comes, someone can continue to war for you even when you aren't connecting with them daily.

2) There are pockets of a friend's life that may not include you. It hurts to think this, but you have to allow those pockets to be just that – portions of her life that may not include you. Don't overthink it. I used to believe that if we were friends, I should know everything, be everything, and be *in* everything. Sadly,

that's unrealistic. Rejection is protection, even if it's for a day or a season. Did it ever occur to you that God knows she is being refined and tested, and the stress level in this season of her life would cause you guys to fight more than ever?

3) Tests like this often come when God sees we have an area in our lives where a seed of jealousy resides. For example, maybe you have a sister, and you felt slighted because she got more attention than you when you guys were growing up, and God knows that's still a sore spot for you. If God sees an opportunity for you to grow, He will put you through a test that requires you to do just that. God isn't a God of games, but He is a God of growth. God has to burn your flesh and peel back those painful layers, and that often comes through testing in the very area you're struggling in. You have to go through, to get through.

> *If God sees an opportunity for you to grow, He will put you through a test that requires you to do just that. God isn't a God of games, but He is a God of growth.*

Anchor Verse: **Romans 12:17 *(TPT)***

Never hold a grudge or try to get even, but plan your life around the noblest way to benefit others.

Scriptures to meditate on: **Job 42:10, 1 Thessalonians 5:11**

War 6 - Warring to Create Space for Her to Grow & Win

Dear Heavenly Father,

Lord, my friend wants to win. I see it all over her and this idea you've given her. She's talked about it so much in the last few months, and I know that she can do it. Father, I ask that You give her the confidence in You to go after what You've placed in her heart. I want to see her move forward in purpose. I pray that I would create a safe space for her to grow and win in our friendship. If she's feeling overwhelmed by all the components of the idea You gave her, help me to be the friend to come alongside her and provide any wisdom that

You may have whispered to me on her behalf. Her evolving doesn't negate anything that I've done. Since I'm still waiting for my dream/business to jump off, I pray that my heart and spirit will be a safe place for her dreams and ideas, and her worries and fears. As she steps forward in faith, trusting You, I pray that You give me the vision to help her see past this point. I pray for a spirit of peace and calm over any anxious thoughts I may have about her growing and not having time for me. She's a champion, and I know that she can handle every blessing that You bring into her life, including the blessing that is our friendship. If this season of growth means that our time connecting may decrease, I ask that You start to prepare my heart. It's resting safely in Your hands, so I don't need to fear being forgotten, overlooked, or neglected. Increase my level of grace so that I will know how to handle when she becomes forgetful, or if she isn't keeping her word to me. Help me charge it to her head and not her heart, knowing that she's never been here before. This is her time to soar and if spreading her wings means a brief season of separation, give me the strength to pour into the relationship I have with You more and more. If she's doing something that may be contrary to what You've called her to do, I pray that even this will be a moment of growth for her. Growing doesn't always mean winning – sometimes it means failing in God and failing forward, so I pray that she will choose growth over opportunity, growth over profit, and growth over comfort in this season. Anything You can do to use me to help add value to her life in this season, reveal it to me so that I may be of support in and out of season the way You feel is best. In Jesus' name, Amen.

The Breakdown

Disclaimer: This chapter and the seasons of disconnect tie together. However, one is when the disconnect happens unexpectedly, and this one is preparing your heart before it happens.

This may seem easy, but the truth is, creating a space for our friends to grow and win can often mean they may grow and win without us in the picture. This isn't because they're being mean or trying to forget us, but because their growth requires something from them that they've never had to do before.

If you started a business last year, but God revealed to you that this year, he wants you to focus on adding an additional service, yet you've never offered that service before, you'd be overwhelmed, correct? You'd immediately jump into research mode, and you'd try to figure out what that would look like for your business. Then, let's say you found out it required you to learn a new skill, so you sign up for a class that helps you develop that skill. As God starts to lead you, you realize you've been focusing so much on your business in the last week that you missed your usual Facetime convo with the bestie.

Not to mention, it's Friday night, and you're running an hour late for your usual friend fiasco at your favorite restaurant. You pick up your phone, and you see three missed calls from her, a voicemail, and several text messages. Exhausted, you call her and explain that you didn't realize time had gotten away from you *and* you're trying to figure all this out, *and* you're feeling stressed; you haven't taken a shower all day (I'm just saying, it depends on the type of work mode you're in), and driving across the city now would mean you're going to be even later. You apologize feverishly, praying that she'll understand. Sounds familiar, doesn't it?

That's what this prayer is about – preparing your heart, mind, and spirit to create the space for your friend to grow and win before she starts her new journey. I'll be honest, that's not always the initial reaction. I mean, you've been waiting for her for an hour, *and* she was home all day working on her business, so at some point, a phone call or text would've been nice – but that's what grace is about. Creating a space for someone to grow and win means you have to ask God what that will look like for you and that particular friendship and ask Him to help you increase your level of grace.

It may be understanding that she has to focus and needs you to send encouragement via texts whenever she crosses your mind, even if she's not able to respond; or it could mean rooting for her as she steps into a new promotion while you're still looking for a job (God may even tell you to give her a congratulatory dinner). It could mean offering to watch her kids even if that means you see them more than you see her. The point is to pray that God would not only bless her while she's progressing but to give you the capacity to handle what that means for your relationship with her.

The point is to pray that God would not only bless her while she's progressing but to give you the capacity to handle what that means for your relationship with her.

Anchor Verse: Proverbs 17:17 (TPT)

A dear friend will love you no matter what, and a family sticks together through all kinds of trouble.

Scriptures to meditate on: **Isaiah 43:18-19; Ruth 3**

Here's Your 1st Challenge.

Scan the QR code to watch your challenge on YouTube.

iPhone: Just open your camera and hold it up to the QR code. The link will instantly come up.

Android: You have to download a QR Code reader app.

War 7 - Warring for Her When She Chooses Wrong

Dear Heavenly Father,

I don't agree with the decisions my friend is making right now. In fact, I know that these decisions are against everything she believes in, everything she stands for, and she often voices those very frustrations to me – that she feels like something is off. So, I'm asking that You give me the tongue of the learned. Help me to realize that even when she chooses wrong, I am not God. I am a vessel. Use me in this season of her life to help remind her of her value and the promises she's made to You and herself. Even if she responds dismissively or nonchalantly, help me to pray without ceasing. Help me to know that every time I pray for her, those are seeds that are being sown into good ground. You hear every prayer that Your children pray, and You honor when we pray in faith. I pray that You would open her eyes to see the error of her ways and to remember that any blessing You send has no sorrow attached to it. I pray that if her heart is heavy and grieved, that she would acknowledge it and bring it to You. I pray that You would close doors that she doesn't have the strength to close. I pray that You would help her to walk boldly in her decisions once she makes them. I pray over every aspect of her business, relationships, friendships, and partnerships. I pray that she would hear Your voice louder than her own fleshly desires. God, help her choose You every time, even if that means those very things she chose would fall off or walk away. Help her to see that when the phone stops ringing and those text messages aren't coming through, that You are protecting her. Help her to know if that contract never reached her email, it's because You heard her prayer, and you didn't want her in that business deal. I'm praying that she keeps You first in all things so that every decision would be filtered through the Holy Spirit. While she may not have done that at the beginning, it's never too late for You to help her choose the right path. You know what decisions she needs to make and how they should look. Help her to make them, Lord. I pray for smooth transitions and disconnections from anyone sent by the enemy. Lastly, I bind the spirit of "I told you so" right now. Help me to trash that from my vocabulary because a real friend doesn't need to be right to see their friend set free. In Jesus' name, I pray, Amen.

The Breakdown

Before you jump the gun, this prayer isn't just about your friend being in the wrong romantic relationship. This is about any decision that she makes where she's being pulled away from the original vision and plan that God has for her life – the things you both have prayed about and things that have been confirmed. This is about when you get a revelation about someone, or something, she's attached to that isn't good for her, but she hasn't yet received that revelation. Here's my first piece of wisdom: Throw away the phrase, 'I told you so.' It's condescending and breeds superiority.

Sometimes, in our haste to see our blessings manifest, we get ahead of ourselves, and we often get ahead of God. Most people don't mean to do that, but the excitement of a new business venture; a mate (finally); that connection in the industry you've always wanted to be a part of; or finally being able to link with that businesswoman you've been following on social media can often lead us to jump before we pray. To be honest, most of the time, we jump and then pray, hoping God meets us halfway through our decision. It's times like this where those very blessings can become more of a burden.

People are going to choose wrong. That's just life. Even you. We all do it. We have to be willing to pray for our friends when they choose wrong, even if she *knows* this isn't the best decision and she's settling. I believe that's when frustrations run deep the most – when your friend says to you, "I know this isn't everything I want, but I'm going to make it work." You remember that scene in Tyler Perry's film, *The Family That Preys*, when Sanaa Lathan's character says, 'Well, I'm just going to enjoy the ride'? She was sleeping with somebody else's husband, and her mother told her that it wouldn't end well, and it didn't.

Even if your friend doesn't say those exact words, you can tell when she isn't happy. You aren't her mother, and we've already established that you aren't God. The best thing to do is pray for her and continue to see her the way God sees her, even if she's lost sight of that herself.

The best thing to do is pray for her and continue to see her the way God sees her, even if she's lost sight of that herself.

Anchor Verse: Proverbs 27:6 (TPT)

You can trust a friend who wounds you with his honesty, but your enemy's pretended flattery comes from insincerity.

Scriptures to meditate on: **Proverbs 24:26, Proverbs 17:9**

War 8 - Warring for Her When She's Being Courted (And I'm Not)

Dear Heavenly Father,

What's up, Lord? Now, my sister and I were both praying for our future husbands at the same time – fasting, believing, standing in the gap for one another, and then – she met her prince charming, and I'm over here flipping through the 'gram (Instagram) praying for a breakthrough. Father, take this jealousy that's trying to rise up and turn it into joy because I know that You're in the neighborhood, and You're about to ring my doorbell. Help me to remember that favor isn't fair, and You have someone amazing for me also. Help me remember not to look to my left or my right when it comes to blessings and increase. My blessings will look different from hers, and vice versa. I pray that she will continue to seek You and that her man of God is honoring her the way she desires. I pray for both of them to remain pure before You, and I pray that she won't do anything that goes against what she believes. I pray for them to continue to invest in their personal relationship with You and that they also pray together. Give my sister wisdom to navigate her new courtship. Help her not to sabotage the blessing You've given her by bringing old mindsets, behaviors, and trauma into this moment. I pray for continued healing over her heart and pray that any old residue is removed from her life. I pray that she daily sits at Your feet and allows You to fill her spirit, heart, and mind. I pray that they don't idolize each other, but that they have a healthy perspective of each other and remember to keep You in Your respective position – FIRST. Help me to remember that Your timing is perfect. I realize that she *and* her mate were both ready. I feel ready, and I pray that You continue to prepare my husband, but there are things I can't fully see and may not know. Therefore, I pray against the spirits of envy, bitterness, and resentment and ask that You give me insight into how I should continue to prepare for my mate while I'm waiting. Speak to my future husband as well. I pray that he be led according to Your will in his preparation process. Help me to lean in and learn from her, now that she is being courted. As they are courting, help me to fill my time with purpose and praise while I wait. Help me to push back against feelings of being left out and give me the strength to push her even more into her new season without feeling like I can't be happy for her. Help me also to remember that you pay attention to how I respond when others receive in the area that I'm waiting on You to fill. Help me to respond well and walk out my season until you're ready for it to change. In Jesus' name, Amen.

The Breakdown

Truth: I was rarely that friend that felt envious of my friends when they got into a relationship. For most of my life, I've been single. I literally enjoyed my twenties and found myself enjoying the freedom of getting to know who I was. I was also still battling mental health challenges, low self-esteem, and other trauma throughout my teen and young adult years, so I was much more interested in dating and having fun (you can translate that for yourself).

The seasons where it was toughest for me being single was when a friend would kick me to the curb while she was in a relationship. However, let me be clear that just because someone feels this way doesn't mean that they are jealous. Most people don't know what to do with those feelings. I'm the friend that understands how to fall back, especially since most of my friends were always in relationships – but I could never wrap my mind around someone losing themselves completely in a guy, especially at a young age. I think that's why I've never been in a real, serious relationship. I've had "situation-ships" and I've had causal relations, but I've never been in anything real serious.

But I know this isn't the narrative for most women. Some women feel challenged in their emotions when they see their friends laughing and smiling with their Bae, and they're still waiting on God to bless them. Some women don't know how to navigate when they feel left behind, especially when their friend is moving forward. I think most women can navigate the space of their friend's career-advancing or even them having a baby first – but because love is such a huge part of life, I believe we as women wrestle with this feeling the most.

Why? Because love makes us feel worthy. Love makes us feel needed and wanted. Love has a way of making life easier, even when death hits. Love has a way of making all the ugliness of the world dissipate at the end of a long day. For the last two years, I've asked God to help me navigate this season of singleness because my desire for marriage has increased. I've felt loneliness constricting at my heart like never before. So, trust me when I say that I get it. Love is beautiful when it meets you, and it's even more beautiful when you know God has placed you together with your mate.

But let's go back to the beginning of this story. I remember saying I wanted to be married somewhere around the age of twenty-five. It's taken me eleven years to walk through healing (God's way) aided by therapy, prayer, His Word, and other valuable resources. One thing I've learned is that God will not shortchange the preparation process to bring you something you want. He prepares the vessel to bring you what you need. Most of us waiting to be courted are being prepared for something we could've never handled in the previous season. Let God do the work He wants to do. I can honestly say I probably would've destroyed whoever my husband is had I met him any time before this moment.

> *Most of us waiting to be courted are being prepared for something we could've never handled in the previous season.*

And before you mention 'dating while waiting,' let me give you some food for thought: Time is valuable – something you can't get back. As women, we naturally love hard and give our all when we build connections. Imagine building a connection with someone you're just dating "in the meantime," and God can't send you the man He has for you because someone else is in his space? Do I think dating is okay? Sure, but only as God leads you to. It should be in the context of knowing that you're dating for a purpose and not to pass time.

Anchor Verse: Exodus 20:17 (NKJV)

You shall not covet your neighbor's house; you shall not covet your neighbor's wife, nor his male servant, nor his female servant, nor his ox, nor his donkey, nor anything that is your neighbor's."

Scriptures to meditate on: **Proverbs 14:30, Job 5:2**

War 9 - Warring for Her Singlehood

Dear Heavenly Father,

I come before You asking You to cover my sister's singlehood today. I know that society and our own timelines often have her fearing this waiting season that she's in, but I pray that she trusts You more and more each day. I pray that whatever strategies she needs to implement to walk boldly in her singleness, that she will do so. I pray against the need to scroll social media and inundate herself with bridal imagery, articles, and stories that would cause her to idolize the idea of marriage. I pray that You lead her to prepare properly for the spouse she is praying for.

I pray that she fills that void with You and You alone. I pray that she recognizes any areas of her life that need healing and a touch from You before she becomes one with someone else. I pray that she would see marriage in a Godly way and not just as a worldly achievement. Give her grace to understand her season of singleness and to maneuver it well. I pray that wisdom and knowledge would find her in this season and that she would grab hold of Your hand as You lead her. Reveal to her the gifts and talents that You've placed on the inside of her that this world needs. Help her to pursue the field that You've assigned to her name, the same way Ruth tended to the field that was assigned to her. Help her to walk in purpose and be more focused on fulfilling those desires You've placed in her heart, rather than rushing you to fulfill the timing of desires that are out of her control. I pray that You give her fresh understanding and insight daily on boundaries to implement for herself in her waiting and for things to do to fill her time. I pray against the spirit of masturbation and the spirit of pornography as she waits in this season. Help her to be committed to purity and Your vision of purity for her life. Help her take her nose out of romance novels and turn her attention away from other forms of entertainment that are falsely feeling that void. Help her to focus on meaningful and purposeful connections. If she has any triggers, help her to identify them.

Help her pray about the doors she needs to close to have a successful season of singlehood. Give her eyes to see this season as a blessing and not a curse. In Jesus' name, Amen.

The Breakdown

I know you were waiting for that chapter that hit right in the gut. Well, so was I. When it comes to singlehood, many of us struggle in this area. You may be the married friend here, so you've walked through that season yourself, and you know what that's like, or you may be the single friend as well, and you guys are waiting together. Whatever position you're currently in, this prayer reveals so much about why waiting well is so important.

1) **Purpose** – There's nothing worse than getting married before identifying your purpose – and then discovering that purpose only to find that the person lying next to you can't help you fulfill that purpose. There are many married couples currently struggling

because they married someone who can't handle the weight of who they are. While you're single, take that time to discover you. The real you. And most of that comes after…

2) **Healing** – God will help you identify the areas in your life where you need healing. Many people take old childhood wounds into their marriages and end up bleeding right onto their spouse. He ends up receiving the leftover residue of trauma that he had nothing to do with. While you're not seeking to be perfect before you get married, you should be seeking to be whole enough to know who you are, who you are not, and what God has called you to do. Healing allows you to see things from God's perspective so you can walk into your marriage not needing that person to be your end-all and be-all.

3) **Gifts and Talents** – Have fun with your singlehood by asking God to reveal to you and your sister-friend the hidden gifts and talents you have yet to discover. You don't have to accomplish everything before marriage, but you should come to the table fulfilled enough that marriage adds value to your portfolio, not defines your portfolio. So many women end up in

marriages too early, having disrupted God's process of preparing them for their earthly purpose. By then, they may find themselves struggling to help him fulfill his while they are still wondering about theirs. Work on those things you love and give your gifts and talents back to God so He can show you what to build from them. Again –work your field and let God run you right into your husband.

> *You don't have to accomplish everything before marriage, but you should come to the table fulfilled enough that marriage adds value to your portfolio, not defines your portfolio.*

Now you can see why waiting well is vital to a successful singlehood journey. Some people wait, but they wait in despair or in frustration. I have literally done so much during my years being single – things that brought me joy and fulfillment that may not have happened had I been married at the time and had to consider someone else in those decisions (for example, teaching for a year in South Korea). Waiting doesn't mean standing still. It means progressing, growing, healing, learning, and becoming the best version of yourself that you can be alone. Marriage will aid you in becoming a better version of yourself but again it's an addition to your portfolio, not the only investment. Pray that your friend (and you if it applies) will find healing, work on her gifts and talents so that God can reveal the profound purpose they have been called to fulfill.

Healing + Gift & Talents = Purposeful Living

And remember, it's not MARRIAGE. PERIOD. It's MARRIAGE, COMMA.

Anchor Verse: Psalm 42:11 (TPT)

So, I say to my soul, "Don't be discouraged. Don't be disturbed. For I know my God will break through for me." Then I'll have plenty of reasons to praise him all over again. Yes, living before his face is my saving grace!

Scriptures to meditate on: **Psalm 68:6, Galatians 6:4, Psalm 138:8**

War 10 - Warring to Value Her & Support Her

Dear Heavenly Father,

When we value those You place in our lives, we learn to see them the way You see them. Help me to value my friend. I can go to all the events she puts on, attend every social gathering she has, and even support her business – but if I don't value her, none of that matters. I don't just want to be a fan traveling alongside her on this journey called life, so show me how to value what You've placed on the inside of her. Show me how to appreciate the oil she carries without feeling inferior to her. Thank You for placing me around her so that I can learn and glean from who she is. Help me to know that having a woman of God like her in my space is priceless. Teach me not to idolize her or her accomplishments, but to value the God inside of her and the God things You are doing in her life. You've chosen her for the purpose You've given her. I pray over that calling and decree that she will fulfill it. I declare that she will step into the fullness of her destiny as You guide her. When she feels overwhelmed and doesn't believe in what she carries, show me how to war for her and do the things You've called me to do to pull that out of her. Help me understand the weight of who she is. As You give me understanding, help me to comprehend with my spirit and then my heart so that I can be of assistance. If I feel that I can't give my all in this season, help me to take a step back until You've refined me. Help me to know that taking a step back doesn't mean stepping off. You give me space to grow, so help me to do the same here. God, help me to realize that You wouldn't place us in each other's lives at this moment unless You had something for both of us. As you reveal to me ways to show her that I appreciate what she offers to the world, also reveal places in me that I should value as well. In Jesus' name, Amen.

The Breakdown

Let me be clear: Support is invaluable. We need support, but I've had friends in the past believe that supporting me was enough. *It's one thing for you to buy what I'm selling, but it's another thing to believe in what I'm selling.* And that's the difference. One, support can come from anyone. Even fans buy music and books to support their favorites. Back in 2016, I remember one of my sister-friends allowed me to live with her in L.A. This was one of my biggest leaps of faith. I'd left my job and was moving in the direction I knew God had called me to take. From the moment we discussed it, my friend was clear in how much she believed in me and valued the gift that God had placed inside of me.

She even expressed that if she didn't think I was a good writer, she would've never invited me to come and try LA out. She said, "Mya, you've got it. I saw it that time I printed your manuscript for you." She recognized that I had something special. Then, there was another instance where I had expressed to a different sister-friend that I was hurt that I didn't have her support when my mother had cancer, and I had experienced a family death back-to-back. After careful prayer, I decided to part ways since some of the negative patterns in our friendship hadn't changed. She shared that because she wanted what was best for me and had my best interest at heart, that should've been enough.

Commercial Break: I will never share something on these pages that I don't believe will give context and understanding to the book. What I share isn't meant to hurt anyone as they're reading, or even to ignite feelings of regret. I have completely walked through healing in these areas, but I'm a writer, and I tell stories. Stories help make even the holiest of points more meaningful. Now, back to our regularly scheduled program.

Here's why that is disheartening on so many levels: When you mention wanting what's best for me, you're essentially saying you *know* what's best for me, and you know what type of support I need. However, if the current support I need is that you be there for me while I'm being there for my mom, then the best thing you can do is *ask me* what I need instead of relying on last season's rhythm of our friendship. As women, especially women of God, we need to break down those barriers that tell us, "I'm doing what I can," when we haven't parted our lips to really ask the person, "What can I do?". When you value what you have with someone, the extra mile is always beneficial.

When you value someone, you invest in them in the way that they need, at the time that they need it. It could be prayers while they're building their next business or watching their children (if you have that grace) while they're working overtime to save money toward their future goals; it could be picking up the phone and calling to check in when you know they're going through hell. It doesn't mean you have to physically be there every day, but there should be some semblance of investing during any given season of their lives.

> ***When you value someone, you invest in them in the way that they need, at the time that they need it.***

And guess what? If you can't – that's okay, too. That's why praying this prayer will help you see where you can grow in this area with her, and if you can't, you step aside and allow God to send in the reinforcements she needs. This was also a key lesson for me in my friendships. I had to value what my girls carried enough to understand that what she has to offer isn't just for me. There will be others that God places in her life, and for me, this meant seasons of falling back if her value was needed elsewhere and fighting hard against the spirit of offense.

Anchor Verse: Romans 12:10 (TPT)

Be devoted to tenderly loving your fellow believers as members of one family. Try to outdo yourselves in respect and honor of one another.

Scriptures to meditate on: **Philippians 2:3-4**

War 11 - Warring for Her Marriage

Dear Heavenly Father,

I come to You asking that You reach down and touch my sister's marriage. I pray for Your divine wisdom over them and that they would hear Your instructions for their marriage with clarity. I come against the spirit of division that would try to keep them walking in offense toward one another and ask that You give them the grace to walk in 1 Corinthians 13. If there are any unresolved issues, I pray that You give them the wisdom to prioritize solutions in the order that they need to be resolved. I pray that their union, which is blessed by You, continues to rest on the foundation that is You. I come against any wicked device of the enemy that would try to make them think that a divorce is an option. I decree that their family will continue to fulfill the purpose and plan that You have for them. Help them both compartmentalize successfully so that their marriage doesn't suffer due to external obligations or relationships. Help them to put each other first, after You. If there are friends, family, and colleagues that don't respect their marriage, help them to disconnect immediately. You blessed them with each other because You know what they need. If there are people who can't see that Lord, I ask that You help them to severe ties peacefully while sending prayer and blessings to those individuals. I pray that they know how to put each other first, even above their parents. Teach them how to uniquely honor their parents while understanding that marriage is meant to leave and cleave. I pray that their loved ones would respect their union enough to demote themselves and not act like they are owed something. Show them how to love one another uniquely and not to compare their love with others. I pray that they know how to fulfill each other's needs and that You'll continue to speak to them about how to make each other happy. More importantly, help them remember that marriage is ultimately about becoming more like Christ and being selfless. In this regard, teach them how to out serve each other. Teach them how to love in their respective love language. Help them not to be dismissive about what the other says as they communicate their hearts and needs to each other. Help them listen through their spirits and hearts so they can correct any behavior that may be hurting each other. I pray that they will always respect each other and speak in love, even when discussing a truth that may hurt. Bless their home and their children. While they're waiting for other blessings that they've been praying for, help them trust Your timing. In Jesus name, Amen

The Breakdown

Demotion. It's an ugly word that so many people think is the worst thing in the world. As previously mentioned, I have learned to demote myself in several circumstances. The main area where I've learned to do this consistently is when a friend gets married. For the longest, I didn't have a word for it, but after reading a blog post it made perfect sense. Demotion is defined as a reduction in rank or status. A lot of women are seeing their girlfriends marry before them. While some can celebrate and even help plan everything from beginning to end, many haven't yet grasped the idea that things changed the minute he proposed.

It doesn't mean you can't be a good friend and show support and love to your friend and her new union – it just means you have to understand that to save yourself any hurt feelings, you'll need to automatically demote yourself. Don't torture yourself wishing you guys could still hang out or whine about feeling neglected and wishing that things didn't have to change. I'm not saying you have to cut off the relationship or remove yourself completely but accept that things are going to be different for her and you.

You can still be a great friend and war for her, war for her children, and even be there when she needs you – because she *will* need you; but respect her new union enough to give her room to grow beyond your friendship and into her new role as a wife. If your friend has been married for some time (let's say a couple of years), then I'm sure by now you see that there's a huge difference in the relationship that you both had. Don't take it as her not loving you or no longer needing your relationship.

Maybe look at it from another angle. Maybe God used your friendship to help her learn to walk in love, how to forgive and fight for a relationship, how to cover someone's dreams and desires, and how to celebrate someone's achievements. Although the relationship with a sister-friend and a spouse is significantly different, the basis of a selfless, loving, and forgiving relationship is the same, especially for believers. The characteristics God desires for all of us to grow in can be developed in any connection we have with people (Galatians 5:22-23).

> *Although the relationship with a sister-friend and a spouse is significantly different, the basis of a selfless, loving, and forgiving relationship is the same – especially for believers.*

Praying for her marriage is a selfless act that shows you value the friendship you guys do have and that you're more than happy for her. You believe that this union will bring her closer to God and closer to the other dreams in her heart. Pray and war for her marriage like it's your own. Never discount the importance of being a prayer warrior for your friend. Even if she doesn't get to talk to you or hang out with you as much, she will forever value your prayers, especially as she starts to see the manifestation of God's goodness in her life.

You also may be the only friend that truly understands how to war for someone. I used to think that since I've been single most of my life, I couldn't add value to a married woman's life. I think much of that came from the church – that old saying that goes, "married women shouldn't be hanging with single women." While that may be true to some extent, this doesn't mean you have to cut off your friend or that she's going to cut you off. Natural growth will always lead to the beginning or end of any old cycles that can't go into the next level. God will always be in the midst of it when it's a change He requires.

The more I pressed into my relationship with God, I found women were coming to me that were single, married, had children, had businesses, etc. Some of these things I've never experienced myself, but what I learned is that when people feel God's presence on your life, they can draw from a well they know is filled with what they need. Stay connected to God and let Him determine the rest.

Anchor Verse: 1 Corinthians 16:14 (TPT)

Let love and kindness be the motivation behind all that you do.

Scriptures to meditate on: **Ephesians 4:2, 1 Peter 4:8**

War 12 - Warring for Her Children

Dear Heavenly Father,

I pray over my sister's children today. I know at times she feels overwhelmed raising them, but I know that You've given her the grace to handle these babies. You know what's inside of her, even if she has yet to see it. I pray over each child she is raising, that they would become everything You intended for them to be. I pray right now that every assignment from the enemy against these babies be canceled. I come against the principalities and rulers of the dark world that would try to plant destructive seeds in them at an early age. I pray that she would use wisdom in covering her children in this area as well. Whether she has one or some, God I pray that she would use Your word to rear them. I pray that she listens to what You place in her heart as it pertains to helping each child. Thank you that You've placed something incredible inside each of them. You know the end from the beginning, so I pray You would bless me with wisdom to assist where and when I can. I pray she and her mate find balance and can raise them together. I pray that You bring clarity to her vision for rearing her children so that she can raise them the way You see fit and not based on what she thinks is best. I pray for a supernatural covering and protection over them. I pray over their schoolwork, their teachers, and their friends. I pray over their mental health and their minds. I pray that any thought that doesn't come from you be refuted and cast down immediately. I pray that no matter how young her children are, they will have an encounter with You that is so powerful, they will know how to wage war for themselves. I pray for peace and understanding between siblings and that Your grace, favor, and mercy would rest on their lives. I pray that her children would use wisdom in who they surround themselves with and that they would not fall victim to any of the enemy's tricks to get them trapped. I pray over every connection, that's it's sent by You and that they will neither stumble nor fall. Bless their endeavors and give them great success according to Your plan and purpose for their lives. In Jesus' name, Amen.

The Breakdown

Never underestimate the power of praying for your friend's children. I have another prayer in this book that talks about praying for her blind spots, in which I talk about praying that she sees things that are going on with her children that the enemy has kept her blind to, but this prayer is focused on the overall view of praying for her children. It can be tweaked to match praying for a single mother.

You don't have to be the designated Godmother to war for your friend's children. The key is to pray over them and continue to keep them covered, especially if you know she leads a busy life. She may be praying over her children daily but could also feel rushed in doing so, meaning she may forget to cover all areas. That doesn't mean you need to know what areas she's covered so you can cover them, it's about being consistent in wanting to see her win in all areas of her life.

Now, more than ever, as we witness black mothers losing their sons at the hands of police, prayer is not to be taken lightly. You never know what kind of seeds your prayers could be planting or what process the enemy has started that your prayers can thwart. Always pray that as she reveals things to you and shares her heart regarding the concerns she has about her children, that you have an ear to hear. Listening with your natural ear is great but hearing with your spiritual ear is *greater*. God often speaks through people's pain, and when someone shares that pain with you, you need to be able to hear correctly.

> *You never know what kind of seeds your prayers could be planting or what process the enemy has started that your prayers can thwart.*

So many mothers also have children that have illnesses. These are the times when praying over her children could make all the difference as it pertains to healing. Mothers are natural heroes, but sometimes, they attempt to wear their capes alone and forget about those other superpowers that they have – God and their village. He may give you the wisdom that she needs, and that wisdom will begin to manifest once you open your mouth in prayer.

I have to be honest. I didn't always know how to do this, especially when my friends would have children, and I ended up not being the Godmother. To be clear, this wasn't something that was pressing for me, but I was raised to know that Godmother's sort of signified being the spiritual parent for a child. I would pray, but my prayers would be aimless. There's nothing that breaks the enemy's agenda down like focused, fortified prayers. Prayers that make hell and the devil nervous because you're on to their game.

Anchor Verse: Luke 18:16 (TPT)

But Jesus called for the parents, the children, and his disciples to come and listen to him. Then he told them, "Never hinder a child from coming to me. Let them all come, for God's kingdom realm belongs to them as much as it does to anyone else. They demonstrate to you what faith is all about.

Scriptures to meditate on: **Psalm 115:14**

Here's Your 2nd Challenge.

Scan the QR code to watch your challenge on YouTube.

iPhone: Just open your camera and hold it up to the QR code. The link will instantly come up.

Android: You have to download a QR Code reader app.

War 13 - Warring for Her to Flourish in Other Friendships

Dear Heavenly Father,

One of the most beautiful things about friendship is that You know exactly who we need and when we need them. You placed my friend in my life because You knew that we both would need what the other has and that we would add balance to each other's lives. There are other women out there that also may need what she has. Help me not to feel slighted because of these new relationships forming. Instead of me agreeing with my feelings or any negative thoughts the enemy places in my mind about these new friends, I pray that You would help me to see them from Your eyes. Even if I know something that my friend doesn't know, I pray You would give me the wisdom to share it in love and only as You leads, not to create division and gossip. If I believe this person does not have my friend's best interest at heart, help me to bring it to You and trust that you are a sovereign God who will reveal it to her as well. Lord, You placed her in my life because You knew her beautiful spirit would help me become stronger and better in some way. I pray that the new women she's developing relationships with would value her and truly be a friend to her. I pray that their relationship is based on You bringing them together during this season and not something that's forced or that has ulterior motives. I pray that her new sister-friends would honor her values, her gifts, and what she has to offer. I pray that there are no feelings of inferiority or jealousy on either end. I thank You that her light shines so bright that many are drawn to her and want to be her friend. Help her to make wise decisions in her new friendships and to set healthy boundaries. Help me respect those boundaries and not feel the need to tag along just because I don't want to be left out. I pray, Lord, that we can carve out our own time and still grow our friendship, regardless of any new ones that come along. I pray that we both can respect each other's "new" and find ways to serve each other without feeling like we're forcing what we have. I also pray that You would help me to flourish in new friendships as well. Every friend that You send has something that we need. I believe that wholeheartedly, so I refuse to fear losing my friend, and I come against anything that would make her fear the same. You close and open doors, so until You say otherwise, help me continue to be a good friend. Help me speak up without fear of rejection, knowing that because we love each other, she will honor me as my heart speaks. In Jesus' name, Amen.

The Breakdown

I get it. It can sting when your sister-friend begins a relationship with someone new, especially if you have a healthy boundary that says, "she doesn't have to include me in her other friendships." When we were all in grade school, it was cute to befriend someone new and then brag about that new friend so we could all hang out at each other's house that weekend. But today - that's not always the case. I'm a firm believer that people shouldn't force friendships. You can grow with another sister-friend without feeling like I have to be friends with her as well, and vice versa. I protect my space and spirit a lot - mainly because I wasn't always responsible in this area and found myself being too trusting, open, and careless with my heart – so I never force friendships (or any relationship).

It can hurt when you feel like you're pushed to the side when your sister-friend gets a new friend or reconnects with an old friend. I've been there so many times throughout so many friendships that I would end up feeling lonely, rejected, and let down. I didn't know how to navigate the seasons where my friends developed new friendships outside of me. So, I said all that to say - when your sister-friend begins to flourish in her other friendships, be careful not to allow the narrative of the enemy to penetrate your spirit and mind. There are always two narratives that present themselves during times like this:

1) We can look at it from what the enemy is trying to do: The enemy wants you to be bitter and resentful toward your friend. He loves division and would hop

at the chance to water any seeds that you take from his grip. He'll try to plant a narrative in your head (a seed) that goes like this: "See? After everything you've been through together and now, she's spending all this time with her. They haven't even invited you to go with them on that trip. Didn't you help her with the kids last weekend? Remember what happened the last time she met a new friend? She only called you when she wanted or needed something, never to check on you. You mind as well cut her off now. This won't end well." Now, before you've even had a conversation with your friend, you've completely taken this narrative and started ruminating over it in your head, again and again – and again. Before you know it, you've deleted her number and unfollowed her on the gram (which is *very* petty, might I add). The enemy's perspective is always thwarted and jacked up. One, he hates unity. He doesn't care if it's a marriage, friendship, business partnership, whatever – he hates unity. If he senses that he can birth division in a relationship, he will. The truth is, most of the time, we give him the right to do so. Once that narrative festers in our minds, and we begin to speak that narrative, he's won. The key is to disrupt any story that doesn't come from God, or…

2) We can look at it from what God is doing: Seasons are beautiful because they're all different. What I appreciate about the seasons, is that each one provides me with different landscapes and backdrops of weather that are meant to bring about beautiful results (for example, April showers bring May flowers). Your friendships are like those seasons. They change. They grow. They sometimes feel stagnant. They may even feel a bit dry, kind of like how our skin feels in the winter months. During that time, God is working something beautiful behind the scenes. Maybe now, you can work more on what He told you to work on – like, that book idea He gave you two months ago? Since you guys aren't on the phone every Sunday night watching and rehashing *The Real Housewives* together, you've got time to write it.

Commercial Break: As you continue to navigate through this book, think of me as your *real* friend. The one who tells you the truth in love and holds no punches; but she's also the one that's walked through every prayer and truth in this book, so I ain't the pot calling the kettle black. K? Now, back to our regularly scheduled program.

Like I was saying, now that you aren't on the phone for two hours every Sunday because she's developing a new friendship – one in which you hope all things go well – you can focus on what you *should* focus on. God is changing both of your seasons, but you only see that you "lost your homie," instead of seeing that God is the homie, in and out of season. Trust the flow of the new season even if the currents are different. God knows what He's doing. He can take what appears to be a sour or bad moment and turn it into something beyond beautiful.

> *God is changing both of your seasons, but you only see that you "lost your homie," instead of seeing that God is the homie, in and out of season. Trust the flow of the new season even if the currents are different.*

Anchor Verse: Proverbs 17:17 (TPT)
A dear friend will love you no matter what, and a family sticks together through all kinds of trouble.

Scriptures to meditate on: **Ecclesiastes 4:9-10**

War 14 - Warring Against the Spirit of Gossip

Dear Heavenly Father,

According to James, chapter 3, Paul talks about the damage the tongue can do. It's a small member but can do a lot of damage and can even set something on fire with its power. I pray against the spirit of gossip in my friendships. Father teach us to know the difference between discussing a situation healthily and productively that will yield fruitful results versus telling someone's business and disclosing sensitive information that doesn't need to be shared. Help us honor and respect any friendships that we have outside of each other and not feel the need to discuss each other's friends. Show us how to be uplifting with our words and to be encouraging without looking for something in return. Teach us how to be sensitive to the needs of the women around us and to support them. Help us not to down another woman or look down on her because she doesn't fit some superficial standard that we may have created in our own mind. I pray that anything that we share with each other will stay in this safe space. I pray that instead of discussing it with others, we pray for one another as we learn to hear from the throne instead of running to the phone. Lord, when either of us starts to gossip, I pray that we can disconnect the conversation in love and that neither of us will be offended. Help us understand that accountability is important. Iron sharpens iron, and if we value what you're doing in our lives, I pray that we'll trust that You can do the same work in someone else, even if we don't see it yet. Forgive us for being judgmental, short-tempered, and intolerant of others that don't look, believe, or act like us. Help us appreciate the differences in others and to know that You hear every word that comes out of our mouths. When we speak of someone who has been created in Your image and likeness negatively, we're just as guilty as someone who may be hurting them physically. Teach us how to not waste time talking and discussing others but to have uplifting, encouraging conversations that speak to healing, growth, and joy. If there's anyone in our space that can't honor this, I pray You give us wisdom on how to have a healthy conversation without hurting anyone's feelings, but to speak the truth in love – and ultimately, disconnect if need be. Teach us what to say and reveal to us when and how to say it. In Jesus' name, Amen.

The Breakdown

Guilty as charged. Don't worry – before I step on your toes and come all up in your house, I'm going to put the spotlight on me. This was me – the friend who discussed my friends with other friends and didn't realize how much damage I was doing behind closed doors. Even though they may not have known each other or had yet to even meet, I learned quickly how God chastises those who choose to use their tongue for evil. I didn't realize how much power my tongue had until God revealed to me that I would use my voice to touch the world. I started to consider how I was handling what He'd given me – the power to change and impact lives with my voice.

Let's define gossip before we go any further so that this chapter can bring you some clarity (by the way, this is the Mya Kay version):

Gossip is anything that you say that would cause division, spread truth, or negativity, causing people to see someone in a negative light – this includes sharing information that you didn't verify or pass through the Holy Spirit.

I didn't realize how much power my tongue had until God revealed to me that I would use my voice to touch the world.

If you wouldn't say it in front of Jesus or that person, it doesn't need to be said. In fact, Jesus may be the only person you should take it to because He's the only person that can help you with that concern or issue. Listen, I *loved* the show 'Gossip Girl.' I've literally watched the whole series twice on Netflix. I never read the books, but when I tell you I loved the show – that's an understatement. I would find myself every week saying, "Man, these people are petty. They sleep with each other and talk about each other like dogs."

Eventually, I asked myself why I was so attracted to the show, and it boiled down to one thing – the drama. It's the same reason we can discuss 'Love & Hip Hop' or 'The Real Housewives of Atlanta' like we know these women and jump to their defense as if we really know what's going on. Drama is enticing. It lures us in and causes us to absorb more poison than we need to.

That's why gossip is dangerous. It creates unnecessary drama and causes pain. Even if the other person never finds out that they were being discussed, think about how rumors spread and how sometimes, we end up finding out months later that it wasn't even true or that we didn't have all the facts. We end up regretting what we said and ultimately what we believed. As it pertains to friendships, I think it's important to note that gossip can exist in every realm of our lives, including our marriages. We have to be mindful of the slickness of the enemy. He's crafty and can take a well-meaning discussion and turn it into an all-out bashing session that ends in butt hurt feelings and offense being driven into hearts like nails into a floorboard.

Listen, sis. I get it. It's hard to share what's going on in your heart and discuss your pain with a friend without making someone you love look like an enemy. For example, you're upset that something happened, and it hurt you to your core. You need to get it off your chest, and you want to seek some advice. It always sounds simple and always starts out that way. So, let's say you do. Let's say you have the conversation with your ace boon coon, and ya'll pray. You might actually feel better, but the issue still hasn't necessarily been resolved.

Later, you decide to have a girl's night at your house, and several of your friends are invited, including the person who you're still walking in offense toward. You might catch the friend that you discussed the situation with side-eyeing the other friend all night and even being short and dismissive toward her. Your friend (the one you confided in) isn't evil, nor is she a bad person – but she's probably now wrestling with the same emotions you were wrestling with when it happened. Your friend is only reacting off of the emotions and feelings that you fed her. Does that make you wrong? No, but there are other layers to it. So, let's break this down from different angles for more clarity:

1) If your friend shares something with you and tells you not to tell someone, your mother includes that someone. I'm best friends with my mom, and she's my prayer partner. So for me, this can be hard, but at the end of the day, she's included in that someone. Now, if your friend knows your mom and she tells her some of the same things she tells you, then that's different; but even then, be mindful when it comes to privately discussing it.

2) Discussing something with the person who hurt you *first* might actually eliminate much of this. If you have the conversation and she doesn't get it, and you feel it isn't resolved, then ask God for wise counsel that has an unbiased viewpoint – someone who doesn't have impartial feelings towards either of you, but you know they have a sound relationship with God and can give you God's view on it.

3) Truly analyze the situation under the Word of God. Did you play a part in anything that's going on between you and the other person? We often skew the

situation to make ourselves look like the flower girl at the wedding and make our friend look like the disgruntled ex who disrupted the wedding. Be honest in your replay of what went on.

4) If you have a dedicated sister-friend that you share everything with, leave it there. Pray before every conversation and then share your heart. We all need a safe space to share our pain, and there's nothing wrong with that – but if you're sharing it with six and seven girlfriends, then that's six or seven different versions of the story floating around. We all don't have the capacity that Mo'Nique had to keep our stories consistent the way my girl did when Hollywood was throwing her shade. In every interview, Mo'Nique kept that thing so consistent it scared me, okay? So, yeah – be wise and only share what God tells you, with who He tells you and when He tells you.

5) To the church and the women and men who make up the church: If the walls of many churches could talk, we'd probably put *Gossip Girl, The Real Housewives,* and tons of tabloids to shame. God is always dishonored when we dishonor one another. From the

pulpit to the pews, let's be mindful of how we use our words, especially as leaders. God understands that we get hurt and experience pain, just like anyone else in the world. He gets it, but He isn't excusing toxic behavior just because He's merciful and understanding. If you feel convicted reading this part, good. Go to God, repent, and ask Him to help you rectify and restore anyone you've hurt through gossip or negative words. The word tells us if we have any offense toward our brother, before we even approach God, we need to go and address the offense. So, do it. Ask for wisdom and let Him guide you. I always pray, "God, I don't care to throw stones. Fix me first. Then maybe, they will see more of You and know they can change too."

You want to know why this chapter was so long? I see this way too much, and it's painful to watch friendships end because women haven't learned how to create a safe space for the women in their lives – the same safe space they cry out to God for. I also remember being the gossip girl in the church. Once God set me free, I found myself extremely saddened at how many people in the body of Christ don't check this behavior. I've checked myself QUICKLY in this area for the last several years and will continue to do so. Remember, the prayer is always: God, help me be the friend I'm praying for you to send.

It's painful to watch friendships end because women haven't learned how to create a safe space for the women in their lives — the same safe space they cry out to God for.

Anchor Verse: Proverbs 16:28 (TPT)

A twisted person spreads rumors; a whispering gossip ruins good friendships.

Scriptures to meditate on: **Proverbs 26:22, Psalms 15:3, Proverbs 18:8**

War 15 - Warring for Our Communication

Dear Heavenly Father,

I want to pray over the communication between me and my friend. Sometimes, I feel she doesn't fully understand where I'm coming from, and if I'm being frank, she probably feels the same way about me. I don't want us to forfeit a great relationship because we didn't take the time to learn and appreciate one another's communication style. Help us to not only learn each other's communication style but to appreciate it. Help us to communicate the way You would have us to as we navigate this friendship. I pray that my friend and I learn to communicate effectively with each other. I pray that we don't downplay what one another says with words like, "it's not that serious" or "get over it." I pray that we're sensitive to what the other needs without feeling the need to be dismissive. I pray for peace and understanding as we learn how to discuss life, pain, challenges, and triumphs with one another. I pray that we respect when we challenge each other in love. Help us not to walk in any offense if a wrong is brought up, but to see it as a growing opportunity to bring us closer to one another. I pray that we respect one another's boundaries as we clearly and effectively communicate what they are to each other. Boundaries are important as they are another way of communicating a need that should be honored. Help us not to see these boundaries as a way to be distant from each other, but rather as a way to fully respect and understand the nature of our friendship. When she communicates to me that she doesn't want to discuss something, help me be a loving and graceful friend that can honor her request. Everything isn't about me, and the minute my flesh tries to make it about me, I ask that by the power of the Holy Spirit, You would help me turn that moment into a prayer request on her behalf. I pray that she can identify anything from her childhood or her upbringing that is keeping her from communicating well. Help her break any chains that are causing her to live restricted rather than free. Lastly, I pray that You help me to communicate my needs as well. Help me be bold as I share my heart about what I need from the friendship without feeling guilty. I pray the spirit of compromise and servanthood over our friendship. Thank You for wisdom on how to navigate this terrain. In Jesus' name, Amen.

The Breakdown

Piggybacking off the previous chapter, communication is essential and key to a strong relationship. Words hurt and more importantly, a word spoken out of season can hurt just as much as poisonous words. This chapter isn't just about the verbal communication between friends, but also being able to successfully pick up on those spiritual clues that tell you what's going on before your friend says a word. It's also about respecting the language that your friend speaks.

For example, I'm a very blunt, hold no punches communicator. I've learned over the years to be gentle in my approach and in my tone. I'm also a very self-aware person. When I communicate, this comes out a bit aggressively, but your girl is working on that. I promise. When sharing my heart with friends or family, I bear all. I don't hold back any details. I'm a writer and storyteller, so most people get it. I love to discuss things and to get it all out.

However, not all of my friends communicate that way. I used to think that friends were holding back and weren't willing to share their hurt with me just because they weren't as descriptive or communicative as I am. I learned that everyone's communication style is different, and not everyone can articulate their pain the way I can. I also learned that it wasn't a slight toward me, and I shouldn't take it as a sign of rejection. I've even been told by the therapist I was seeing in 2020 that I'm much more aware of my feelings and emotions than many of her other clients.

With this understanding, I've learned how to respect and appreciate that everyone doesn't communicate this way. That's why you have to pray about communicating with your friends. You may take her silence as ignoring you when she's trying to navigate her own feelings about something that happened. You may take the fact that she went to another friend with her pain instead of you as her not needing you, without realizing that maybe that person went through the same thing and she needs a mirror for her pain right now – not a resolve. You could even interpret her distance as neglect when she's truly trying to wrap her mind around what she's experiencing. Perhaps she's trying to keep from turning back to any addictions or old habits that would normally help her numb the pain.

I say this to encourage you. Ask God what your communication style is, and then ask Him to give you the words to articulate that to your friend. Then, find out what hers is. Now, that doesn't mean a time won't come where you both will have to sacrifice and compromise some so that the relationship can work. She may need to acknowledge that you want to feel included in her journey because you know that God called you to her life in this season while you may need to acknowledge that when she's ready to share her heart, she will include you.

> *That doesn't mean a time won't come where you both will have to sacrifice and compromise some so that the relationship can work.*

Anchor Verse: James 3:2 (TPT)

We all fail in many areas, but especially with our words. Yet if we're able to bridle the words we say we are powerful enough to control ourselves in every way, and that means our character is mature and fully developed.

Scriptures to meditate on: **James 3**

War 16 - Warring for Her Boundaries

Dear Heavenly Father,

I come to You asking that You help my friend set up clear, wise, and consistent boundaries with the people in her life. Not just boundaries for those she may not necessarily care for because those are easy, but those that include people closest to her heart. I'm praying that she recognizes the boundaries that she needs to erect in her relationships, workplace, and business. I come against the spirit of fear that would make her feel like erecting boundaries would cause her to lose the people she loves. I pray that she would know the difference between boundaries and walls and that she is wise in expressing her boundaries.

Give her wisdom to know what relationships are draining her or stretching her beyond her capacity in this season. Then, give her wisdom and knowledge to implement what You tell her to. I pray that she understands that anyone who can't respect her boundaries, her 'no' or her needs in this season, needs to be let go. I pray for a smooth transition from those individuals now. I know that in marriage, boundaries are different. I pray that she and her husband understand how to navigate their individual needs and desires without hurting one another's feelings. Outside of that, Lord, I pray that the boundaries that she has to put in place will also be honored by me. Help me not to assume that I am to have access to every area of her life, nor am I to force my way into those areas. If she tells me that she needs time to herself, help me honor and respect that request. Help me and her establish healthy boundaries for our relationship and to maneuver those boundaries well. I pray for divine wisdom and instruction so she will know how to express herself well during this season. I pray that she waits for Your timing on when to have conversations with those in her life who need to be aware of these boundaries. Thank You for giving her a resounding peace as she makes decisions that help her to best honor You, her needs, and the season she's currently in. In Jesus' name, Amen.

The Breakdown

I think if every woman had this prayer in her arsenal when she first started to learn the meaning of what friendship is, she would've had healthier friendships from day one. But most of us learned friendship in the sandbox at the playground or in our first classroom setting in pre-K, so I get it. Boundaries could be the difference between you having a solid and respectful relationship with your sister-friends versus having a rocky and frustrating relationship with your sister-friends.

It wasn't until my late twenties that I learned that I wasn't always going to be let into every area of a friend's life. I think that far too often, we assume that best friends or sister-friends are supposed to tell us everything, let us in on everything, share their childhood trauma with us *and* tell us their whole life story for us to feel like we're really friends. Why is that? I think it's just human nature. We want to feel needed and be seen as the expert that can handle our friend's entire world, whether we admit it or not. However, it's important to pray over your friend as they set boundaries, especially because your heart has to be prepared if those boundaries will change the dynamics of your friendship.

You will also need to set boundaries that speak to your values and your heart's desires. About a year ago, a friend of mine had an outing for her birthday that included going to a haunted house. Anyone who knows me knows that I will not participate in anything involving darkness, or that can open my spirit to the demonic realm. In the past, she and I would go to the movies and enjoy some pretty scary films. Not to mention that growing up, I was addicted to horror and scary movies.

But over the past few years, God has matured me in this area to understand that it's not "just a movie" or "just music." I've had to be "on purpose" about the things that I allow into my atmosphere. With that being said, I called her and had a conversation with her about it in a loving, clear, and detailed way. You may think this was easy, but I want you to get a clear picture: I felt guilty that I could possibly let her down. She had just helped me transition back home to Philadelphia and helped me secure a job. This is where faith and love come in and where you have to trust that by honoring God, He'll have your back no matter what happens.

While I wasn't sure what kind of reaction I would get, I was confident that pleasing God and setting this boundary was important to me. The conversation ended up being blessed and went over well. She was very understanding and respected that boundary. What I ended up being able to do is throw her a surprise dinner at a nice restaurant. At that time, I had no idea she had never had a surprise for her birthday, especially since I spent several years living in different cities throughout our adult years. It wasn't until she texted me the next day telling me how much it meant to her that I realized how God had moved.

Boundaries don't guarantee someone won't be offended or even let down. They do, however, establish a precedent for the way things will be on both ends. Support your friend and the boundaries they set. If you value the friendship, you'll put your selfish desires away and understand it from her point-of-view. Instead of feeling slighted by her boundaries, appreciate the idea that you can help her implement them, and offer to be an accountability partner for her until she's comfortable in this area on her own.

> *Instead of feeling slighted by her boundaries, appreciate the idea that you can help her implement them.*

Possible Boundaries that may need to be implemented:

1) **Friendships** – You aren't obligated to be involved in the relationships she has outside of you, and neither of you are obligated to befriend the other's friends. That's a clear boundary that needs to be discussed and respected. As long as there is respect, love, and there is no gossiping or backbiting, there's no reason why your friendship can't flourish outside of other friendships.

2) **Mates and Marriages** – Nothing you tell your friend should be said to her mate and vice versa, especially if they aren't married. Be sure that when you guys discuss things, she's clear on how you feel about her discussing it with her mate. **Bonus:** When it comes to your friend's mate, all text messages and phone calls to a spouse, outside of planning a surprise for the friend, should take place in a group chat. Period.

3) **Money and Finances** – I speak on this in a full chapter, but outside of three or four times, I was never one to borrow money from friends. This needs to be discussed before a problem arises. Be respectful and honor each other's wishes in this area. One time, I told a friend after she loaned me money that I would prefer to preserve our friendship so we wouldn't have any misunderstandings in the future. Her response was that she wanted me to have the friendship and any monetary support I needed. I had to stand firm. We had already had a bit of a miscommunication in this area, and I didn't want to face that again. Stand firm no matter what, even if the boundary isn't fully understood at first. It'll make things a lot easier in the long run.

Anchor Verse: Proverbs 22:28 (TPT)
The previous generation has set boundaries in place, don't you dare move them just to benefit yourself.

Scriptures to meditate on: **James 1:19, Proverbs 18:13, Proverbs 25:28**

War 17 - Warring Against Feelings of Jealously

Dear Heavenly Father,

I hate feeling like this, but I know that You want me to be honest with You about everything. I want to see my friend happy, but it hurts me to know that I've been waiting for so long for my blessing. You tell us not to covet our neighbor's things, and You don't want us to idolize anything, so help me remember You are a sovereign God who makes no mistakes.

I pray against this spirit of jealousy and ask that You help me to stay focused on You. Help me be grateful because I was praying for my friend to receive exactly what she prayed for.

This doesn't mean You love me any less or that You don't see me. It's just not my time. Help me to realize that and not take this as a slight toward me. You have enough blessings for all of Your children, and You don't owe me anything. Help me see past my own desires to understand that she was ready for this and that she was prepared. I denounce the feelings of contempt and frustration that are trying to overpower my joy. I choose to celebrate her while I'm waiting for my breakthrough. Teach me to wait well. Teach me to serve while I'm waiting. I close the door to the enemy's schemes and tactics that would try to tear this friendship apart because of my selfishness. Give me the strength to be a true friend. If I feel this way, this means You still have work to do in me. This is a true test of my character and my faith. Help me to pass this test. In Jesus' name, Amen.

The Breakdown

Warring on a friend's behalf is tough when you're still sitting in the waiting room. You ever have a friend that calls you crying and complaining about not getting any sleep because the baby was up all night, but you've just had a miscarriage? You remember praying for her and believing God with her, only to be on the other end of a painful loss that you can't even put into words. You want to be the good friend that supports your friend in her season of winning, but you can't ignore the pain that's in your own heart.

You also feel like she could be a bit more sensitive to the fact that you did just lose your baby, and you're trying to wrap your mind and heart around hearing her baby cooing in the background. Listen – if there's any woman that tells you she's never experienced feelings of jealousy when her friend is in a fruitful season, and she's still barren (not just in-regards-to childbearing), you need to remove her from your space because she's lying (no – but she is).

Here's an area I still struggled with as it pertains to jealousy: I've always been a loner, yet I'm an extreme social butterfly. I always knew somebody, and no matter where I traveled throughout Philly, I found myself having plenty of friends. As I got older, somewhere around my mid-twenties, things shifted for me. I think at that point, God knew that if He didn't start to place a protective bubble around me, I would end up not fully surrendering to His plan and purpose for my life.

While I have had an amazing friendship for over thirty years, we still had plenty of seasons where we were both living out God's will for our lives, so we weren't always connecting regularly. So, I spent years feeling like I had no friends or like I couldn't connect with the friends I had. As I continued to live in different cities, God would lead me to beautiful connections, but I felt like I had to watch people win in friendships while I was losing. I would feel my heartstrings pulling when I thought about why people weren't checking on me, reaching out to me, or inviting me to go out. Of course, this was all about my perception at the time.

By the way, let me make something clear: I did put myself out, extending the olive branch and going out of my way to try to make the connection first. It wasn't until two years ago that I realized that the anointing on my life is so valuable that God won't let me be connected with just anyone. I say that humbly and still with a bit of pain because it doesn't change that this is still a bit of a sore spot. I've had to trust God's idea of friendships for me more than what society says friendship looks like in order for me to stay focused.

> *I've had to trust God's idea of friendships for me more than what society says friendship looks like in order for me to stay focused.*

Commercial Break: God has revealed this invaluable truth to me about myself (something that I had to really come to grips with, and I'm paraphrasing here): "You have learned to fill your life with so much of Me, that anyone who encounters you that can't handle that light, won't befriend you. Those who are meant to be in your life will appreciate that light and will be drawn to it. Those who would rather enjoy the sentiments of darkness will not. I will lead you to your tribe, and they will be able to handle the full weight of who you are." Now, back to our regularly scheduled program.

Now, this may not be the same truth that God reveals to you, but either way, you'll have to combat those feelings of jealousy and meditate on God's word, but don't be so hard on yourself. Can happiness and sadness exist in one's heart at the same time? Absolutely. There are times where a quiet demeanor can be misread for everything but what it is - a silent cry for your moment to arise and for the desires of your heart to be fulfilled. I can be happy for you and sad for me without being cast as a bad friend. The key is to not let that sadness grip your heart so much that you fall into depression about something you don't have or where you can't celebrate your friend. It's at that moment that you must surrender your heart's desire for the desired blessing to Him. Turn it into a prayer request, praise Him, and continue to ask the Holy Spirit to reveal the areas where you need to prepare for what you're asking for.

> *I can be happy for you and sad for me without being cast as a bad friend.*

Anchor verse: James 3:16 (TPT)

So wherever jealousy and selfishness are uncovered, you will also find many troubles and every kind of meanness.

Scriptures to meditate on: **James 4:2-3, Romans 12:21, Galatians 5:22-23**

War 18 – Warring to Understand Her Capacity

Dear Heavenly Father,

I'm coming to You asking for You to help me understand my sister's capacity in this season. I do feel left out and somewhat let down. This isn't a prayer about frustration, anger, or jealousy. This is a sincere prayer asking that You help me understand what she can give in this season and what she can't. Maybe she doesn't even know, so forgive me for placing that pressure on her. If this is a season where I will be supporting her more than she's supporting me because her responsibilities have increased, then please reveal that to me and give me the consistency and fortitude to put my feelings to the side for now and be supportive. I trust You with my heart, and I thank You that You're helping me see that friendships require nurturing and care just like any other relationship. Show me the resources and tools I can use in this season to be a better friend. Give me the timing to express my concerns and my heart as You lead. Help me to remember that everyone has a season where they are busier, more focused, and where things change. This doesn't make my needs less important, so help me trust that You have someone on standby ready to be a great sister-friend to me. I thank You for showing me those in my space that can pour into me as well. If this is her season of receiving, make that clear. As she receives from me, I can receive from those You send into my life during this season. Thank You for helping me understand the weight of what is on her plate. I pray for wisdom, love, and grace. Show me how to truly lay down my life for my friend the way You did for me. In Jesus' name, Amen.

The Breakdown

Can I raise my hand now before you even read this chapter? I am the first person to admit that there were so many seasons where I found myself overanalyzing a friendship and whether or not I needed it, all because I wasn't receiving the support I needed. Too often, we feel like a friend is neglecting us, or we feel let down because things have shifted unexpectedly. There's so much that comes with this, but in a nutshell, I had to understand that one's capacity changes in every season.

What was possible in one season might be different in another season. The support doesn't necessarily leave, but it does adjust. I've always been pretty understanding in this area, but it still doesn't mean God didn't have to perform heart surgery on me. The spirit of rejection would hover over me greatly, and I had to learn to rebuke that spirit when it came up. I'm a firm believer in balance, but sometimes balance is simply consistency and commitment. It's not always going to be time well spent in each other's presence. Today women are more understanding than ever that we have to be innovative with the way we connect with each other, and value that the one-on-one time may turn into a group outing due to other commitments and obligations.

> *I'm a firm believer in balance, but sometimes balance is simply consistency and commitment.*

Now, I do believe in the saying that "you make time for what you want." However, I also believe we have to understand that capacity plays a large role in that. No matter who you are or what you do, if you're asking God for great quality friendships, you're going to have to sacrifice something to have and maintain those friendships. Some women feel like they have all the friends they need, and some feel like their husband or mate is their best friend, so anything extra is just that – extra. There are also women longing to build a bond with someone without having to sacrifice their own need for support, love, and consistency.

You know what you can handle and what you can't. Marriage and children don't make friendships any less necessary, but as a single friend, maybe you need to demote yourself and understand that God knows what you need just as much as He has provided your friend with her needs. I think the worse thing anyone desiring a great friendship can do is place a false expectation on someone.

If you know that someone can't be the kind of friend you've been praying for, then move on gracefully. You can love and support a woman without feeling bound to a friendship with her. The key is to pray for understanding and grace so that you can navigate that bond or friendship well.

Anchor Verse: Acts 20:35 (TPT)

I've left you an example of how you should serve and take care of those who are weak. For we must always cherish the words of our Lord Jesus, who taught, 'Giving brings a far greater blessing than receiving.'

Scriptures to meditate on: **Hebrews 13:16, 2 Corinthians 12:9, James 4:6**

Here's Your 3rd Challenge.

Scan the QR code to watch your challenge on YouTube.

iPhone: Just open your camera and hold it up to the QR code. The link will instantly come up.

Android: You have to download a QR Code reader app.

War 19 - Warring for Her Mental Health

Dear Heavenly Father,

I pray over my sister's mental health today. I pray and war against every principality that is trying to cause her to fall into depression. Every principality that causes her to think anxiously and trying to break her focus, I command it to stand down now. I pray peace over her mind and declare that she will think about those things that are true, honorable, good, worthy of praise, righteous, honest, and pure. I decree a sound mind according to Your word in 2 Timothy 1:7. I denounce every mental assignment that the enemy has tried to erect in her life and declare wholeness and healing from the stem of her brain to the top. I thank You that everything she's going through will work out for her good, so there's no need for her to worry or to fear. I pray You'll keep her in perfect peace as her mind stays on You. Give her the reassurance that You haven't forgotten her or the things that she's dealing with. I pray a fresh anointing over her mind and decree that not one thought will be able to keep her from living her best life in You. If she's feeling anxious, I decree she will turn every anxious thought into a prayer request. I pray that she will lift up her eyes to the hills from which all her help flows. God, because You're a good provider and You care about all the needs of Your children, I decree that she now feels her strength being renewed and it will be renewed day by day. If there's anything that she's attached to that is bringing on thoughts of anxiety, fear, or depression, I pray she has the strength to cut it off and shut it down. Cancel the effects of any mental illness that may have been in her bloodline that she's unaware of. I pray that nothing will hinder her from being able to think and meditate on Your Word and Your goodness. When she is feeling weak, I pray Your divine strength over her. I pray that the Holy Spirit will swoop in and help her to think on Your word. I wage war against everything that is waging war against her. I decree that she has the mind of Christ. In Jesus' name, Amen.

The Breakdown

Mental health has become such a huge topic in the last ten years or so. People have been more open to discussing their battle and challenges with mental health. For many, this does not come without a cost. Opening the door for people to have a bird's eye view into your mental anguish is nothing to take lightly, which is why I understand most people not wanting to discuss it. However, it doesn't mean we shouldn't. Believe it or not, mental illness is more common than people think, and many people who suffer from some kind of mental illness have come to realize that it's been in their bloodline for years.

This prayer is about warring for your friend's mind whether or not she's dealing with depression or anxiety. We need to pray to have power stored up for times we need it, not pray when we're in a state of emergency. I've shared on my podcast (The Girl Files, Season 1, Episode 1) about the challenges I faced in college regarding mental illness. I battled greatly with depression and even struggled with thoughts of suicide. I suffered in silence for a little while but eventually stepped up and sought help.

> **We need to pray to have power stored up for times we need it, not pray when we're in a state of emergency.**

I knew that I needed to talk to someone, or I would end up dying early. To be honest, what held me back the most was being afraid of what people would say. The whispers about me being "crazy" were more frightening than what I was actually dealing with.

While I never received an official diagnosis, I don't think it takes a rocket scientist for someone to know that something is disconnected in their mental health. As I sought counseling, therapy, and Godly resources to pull me through, I began to identify the tricks of the enemy and learned how to fight spiritually. The war is always spiritual first, then practical. Your friend may be battling some things that she doesn't know how to put into words, or she may be afraid to. Nobody wants to be thought of as crazy or automatically directed to a medication when they share their pain regarding mental anguish.

The one thing you don't want to do is assume. Until your friend shares with you that she feels something is off, you don't need to become a doctor. With that, I do believe we've allowed therapy and medicine to take the place of Christ in many areas where He offers healing and breakthrough. I'm not saying don't take your medicine or don't get the help you need in the natural, but our first response should always be prayer and The Word. God has a unique plan of healing for everyone, and He is the ultimate healer.

Any regimen or healing process that doesn't include Him will only lead to temporary results and more anguish down the line. Christ is the anchor of all healing, and everything we do should be rooted and established in Him. Keep warring for her in this area, even if she doesn't know what's going on. I've stated this before, but God may reveal things to you that He hasn't said to her, or she may be so

> *Any regimen or healing process that doesn't include Christ will only lead to temporary results and more anguish down the line.*

bogged down with her own stuff that she can't hear God clearly. Wage war for your friend. Her sanity may be depending on it.

Anchor Verse: 2 Corinthians 10:5 (TPT)

We can demolish every deceptive fantasy that opposes God and break through every arrogant attitude that is raised up in defiance of the true knowledge of God. We capture, like prisoners of war, every thought and insist that it bow in obedience to the Anointed One.

Scriptures to meditate on: **Romans 12:1-2, 1 Corinthians 2:16**

War 20 - Warring Against Her Health Challenges

Dear Heavenly Father,

With every diagnosis that we face, You're already in the doctor's room. You knew this health challenge would arise, and You knew who my sister would need to share it with to get the spiritual and physical support she needs. First, we thank You for being a healer. We thank You that Your promises are 'yes' and 'amen.' You have the final say. Until You say it's over, it's not over.

I thank You for the wisdom she needs to change her diet, remove any elements of stress, and anything else that You reveal is needed in this hour. I pray for divine wisdom from heaven for what she needs to implement and what she needs to remove to see Your power work through this situation. I pray she takes steps toward her healing by being consistent in whatever You reveal to her to do. If medication is required, I pray right now that the medication would only do what it's supposed to do. I cancel the assignment of any side effects right now. I thank You that her body is supernaturally covered by Your spirit, so she will not become addicted to any medications but will use them only as they're prescribed. Thank You for her divine healing. Help her to step back from anything that she needs to. I pray that if there are people who need to step up to the plate, they would play their part so that she can truly rest without concern. We thank You now for every strategy you will give her to beat what's trying to beat her. In Jesus' name, Amen.

The Breakdown

There are times health issues come out of nowhere, and it helps to have a prayer handy when you can't think of what to say. Cancer diagnoses, fibroid issues, heart, and thyroid issues are all plaguing many women. It's painful to see someone you love going through such hard times. In this chapter, I would like to shed a little light on sacrifice. Someone I'm connected to has a best friend that recently passed from cancer. To respect their privacy, I won't disclose too much, but I will say this. She not only supported her friend through everything – taking her to treatments and helping with her children, even while raising a child of her own – but during the last year or so of her life, she moved her in with her to support her as her health further declined.

That takes commitment. Real commitment. She works full-time, has a child to raise, and has a side business, yet she found the space and capacity to be a real friend and help someone she loved. If "lay down your life for a friend" was a picture, this would be it. I'm sure this didn't come without challenges, some fights, and even times where she wanted to give up – but to make that kind of sacrifice and not even think twice, is commendable. I also believe if the shoe was on the other foot, she would've received the same support and love.

While not every friend can do this (this goes back to knowing your capacity), the point is to stop and assess your life for a minute. Ask God how you can truly serve in your friend's moment of suffering. No matter how minor or major the health challenge is, it's still scary. There are two things we face in life that usually bring us fear and frustration – money issues and health issues. Never dismiss a health issue because you feel it's "not that major" or because "your favorite auntie had it, so your friend will be fine."

Our bodies tell us when something is off, and until we know what that is, it's likely we'll run through a bunch of things in our minds, and Google will really become our best friend. First time experiences are new, and they scare us until we know that we have no reason to really be afraid. Even the strongest, most faith-driven person falls into seasons of doubt and despair when health challenges arise. Never assume you know the level of your friend's strength just because she's been strong in other areas. Even if you've had a personal journey through the same health issue, know the difference between testifying to God's goodness and dismissing the weight of what she's carrying.

> *Never assume you know the level of your friend's strength just because she's been strong in other areas.*

Anchor verse: Jeremiah 30:17a (NKJV)

For I will restore health to you, and heal you of your wounds,' says the LORD…

Scriptures to meditate on: **Exodus 15:26, Deuteronomy 7:15, Psalm 34:19**

War 21 - Warring for Her Wholeness/Healing

Dear Heavenly Father,

I'm praying for Heaven to meet my sister as she deals with the reality of her pain. Through recent discussions and discovery, she's shared how much she realizes that past hurts have followed her into adulthood. Her life is falling through the cracks right now, and she needs immediate help. I'm praying for her heart, her mind, and her spirit.

May her spirit man rise up in this hour. I pray for wisdom as to how she should handle this situation. I pray that she will first encounter Your presence and divine power. I pray that she is led to Godly counsel who will walk with her through this challenging time. I know I don't have all the answers, so help me pray and support in any way that I can, then step back and allow You to do the work in her. Father, I plead the blood over her from the inside out. Reveal the childhood wounds that have kept her bound and chained. Touch her mind and open up the places where strongholds are keeping her in cycles of destructive behavior. I pray that the enemy is exposed. Every area he has kept in the darkness, hidden away from Your touch, I decree a spirit of exposure right now. Expose those areas so that You can heal them. I come against anything that would disrupt her healing. Cover her from the crown of her head to the soles of her feet. Anybody that wouldn't be able to truly assist her in her healing, I ask that You remove them from her space. Raise up her village to pray for her harder than they ever prayed for her before. God, I thank You that when this season is over, she will be a brand-new person, able to truly walk-in strength and power because of Your hand on her life. In Jesus' name, Amen.

The Breakdown

Some of us have walked through so much trauma that we have no idea how it's affecting our lives. Much of our trauma happened throughout childhood and carried itself into adulthood. There are a lot of hurting children walking around in grown people's bodies. Carrying the burden of trauma has many people thinking that they are just "being strong." Strength isn't ignoring your scars and plowing through life, going from one task to the next while barreling through hardships. Real strength is walking in the reality that you have weaknesses and hurts that have shaped who you are, yet you don't let them define who you are. You realize that what makes you strong will help you play the hand you've been dealt with wisdom but having strengths doesn't erase weaknesses.

> *Real strength is walking in the reality that you have weaknesses and hurts that have shaped who you are, yet you don't let them define who you are.*

Your undealt with hurt and pain is draining the strength you do have. Before I encountered full healing in my life, I was so broken that anyone I connected with I ended up cutting. Even with my best intentions and a heart of gold, my trauma was causing me to push away good people in an attempt to make "bad" people pay. Mental anguish and silent cries that went unheard caused me to lash out at some of the greatest people God placed in my life. For those who stayed and loved me through it, God bless them. I needed that. For those who walked away, God bless you, too. I get it.

What often happens when we continue to sit in our trauma rather than dealing with it head-on is – we take it out on people who have nothing to do with that past experience. Wholeness requires some real deep work and most people aren't willing to get "cut" by God to experience the healing they need. When you see your friend pushing people away or going through constant bouts with pain and heartbreak, it's time to take a step back from 'sip and paints' and grab her hand to travel to a counselor or therapist.

Here are a few signs that will let you know your friend is crying out for help:

1) Constantly making statements about people not understanding them and wanting a break from people

2) Isolating themselves or withdrawing from life to the degree that they need to be reminded or nudged to handle their responsibilities

3) Being extremely snappy or irritable in circumstances or situations that aren't severe or a real threat to their life and safety

4) Crying constantly without being triggered

While this isn't an all-inclusive list, these are things I dealt with and wished that at the time, someone knew how to listen. I battled with this severely in my twenties, and except for a few people knowing, I suffered in silence. Most people don't know how to put a name to their pain and don't know how to describe what they're going through, but you can be supportive without knowing all the details. Never underestimate the power of spiritual insight. Too often, we pray for wisdom, insight, and understanding, then we receive it and chalk it up to us overthinking. I'd rather ring my friend's phone to show I'm deeply concerned and have her tell me to leave her alone than to get a different kind of phone call later because I didn't answer the promptings of the Holy Spirit.

Commercial Break: If you've ever experienced this kind of pain, do not let the spirit of guilt overflood you right now. I rebuke it on your behalf. I'm speaking as a woman who experienced suicidal thoughts and depression severely throughout my twenties. I wish someone had stepped in and called me that way because there were times that I wasn't sure if I would make it through. Today, I want to be that overly concerned friend, and I pray you will be as well.

Anchor verse: Psalm 32:7 (TPT)

Lord, you are my secret hiding place, protecting me from these troubles, surrounding me with songs of gladness! Your joyous shouts of rescue release my breakthrough.

Scriptures to meditate on: **Proverbs 1:33, 1 Peter 5:7, Isaiah 53:5**

War 22 - Warring for Her Parents

Dear Heavenly Father,

I come to You asking You to keep and protect my sister's parents. She's dealing with the weight of being a caregiver, and sometimes, her parents forget that she has other responsibilities. My prayer is that You would first help them rely on You more than they rely on her. Give her the grace and wisdom to have conversations with her parents can set healthy boundaries and give them peace in any decisions that need to be made.

I ask that You protect their minds against the tricks and tactics of the enemy. Lord, I pray her parents would allow her to grow into her own dreams and purpose as she balances being loving and supportive to them. I pray healing in any areas where they may be afflicted and ask that You give them insight into healthier eating habits and how to take better care of their bodies. Father, as her parents get older, I pray that she would be able to support them with the means that You've given her. She is a good, loving, and caring daughter. In-regards-to her mother, I pray that her husband and children continue to call her blessed well into her old age. I pray that her father would continue to be the loving and protective man of God you created him to be. Thank You, Lord, for the wisdom that her parents provide, and I pray that they have a safe space to share their wisdom and knowledge without feeling like a bother. I pray that they respect the way she chooses to live her life and do things. I pray that they will not make her feel obligated to carry on any family traditions that she doesn't want to carry on. While loving and honoring our parents is a commandment, we are not obligated to live life for them, so I pray that You give my sister peace with all decisions that she makes to honor and obey You. If she is embarking on a journey contrary to the vision her parents had for her, I pray that You would give her the strength to obey You over them. Her life belongs to You. You know what she needs and what You've called her to do.

Your word makes it clear that we are to leave everyone to follow after You and pursue Your will, so I pray against the spirit of selfishness in her family bloodline and pray a spirit of peace and understanding. In Jesus' name, Amen.

The Breakdown

This one is tough. For those of us who love our parents fiercely, it's hard to balance doing what we know is right in our hearts versus what they want us to do. It's so easy to tell a friend what they should and shouldn't do. That's why this prayer carries so much weight. Everybody's dynamics with their parents is different, and everyone's upbringing is different, even if there are some similarities. People are often afraid to make decisions for themselves for several reasons:

1) They feel they owe their parents for the things they did for them (and their parents may express this in a plethora of ways), *or…*

2) They believe they're indebted to their parents because they messed up a lot and their parents always bailed them out of trouble, *or…*

3) The enemy has plastered so much guilt over their lives that they don't realize their parents actually long for them to live their own lives.

When I first moved to Atlanta at the age of twenty-seven, it was my first-time leaving home. I had never lived outside of Philadelphia. My mother had only been cancer-free for about two months when I left. I was excited and thrilled to take such a huge leap. After a couple of months of being in Atlanta, my mother ended up going to the hospital for an allergic reaction she had to a medication she was taking. She was there overnight. The weight of guilt and depression that hit my life wreaked havoc for about six weeks.

Even after she was home and doing better, I found myself stressing over the fact that I had left home. She was doing fine, but the enemy had plagued me with so much guilt that I couldn't see that God had answered my prayer – which was to heal her quickly. I milked a whole twenty-four hours and turned it into several weeks – all because I didn't exercise the authority God had given me. I hear so many stories of people not leaving home or separating from their parents because they're afraid of what will happen if they go.

> *I milked a whole twenty-four hours and turned it into several weeks – all because I didn't exercise the authority God had given me.*

I can't speak for everyone, but God has revealed quite a bit to me since I took my first leap of faith. I am not my mother's Savior. The underlying fear in me not wanting to leave had nothing to do with her being sick – it was about me feeling like she needed me to be there because she was lonely. My mother and I are the best of friends, and I value and cherish that, but God had to give me a reality check when it came to this. A lot of it was pride, as if my mom couldn't make it without me. I feared separation. And there's nothing wrong with that, but if it keeps you from obeying God and pursuing what's in your heart, you're living in disobedience.

Your friend may very well be struggling in this area. She could be married with children or a single mom and can't ever seem to stand up to her mother, or her father may run off every guy she dates, and she's in her thirties…whatever the dynamic, it's important to understand this: Being a daddy's girl and being best friends with your mother is a blessing, but there must be a balance that she has, or she'll live with resentment and contempt in her heart.

Pray this prayer as much as she needs, especially if she's in a current situation where she feels caught between a rock and a hard place (i.e. her husband and her parents, etc.).

Anchor Verse: Ephesians 6:3 (TPT)

"You will prosper and live a long, full life if you honor your parents."

Scriptures to meditate on: **Ephesians 6:4, Deuteronomy 6:1-3**

War 23 - Warring for Her Healing & Dealing with Loss

Dear Heavenly Father,

My sister's heart is breaking due to the loss of her loved one. First, help me to control my tongue and what I say. Help me not to just quote scripture or speak cliches that sound good at the present moment. Help me to listen with my ears and my heart to what she needs. I pray for comfort and peace over her as she struggles with this loss. If there is anything that I can do that she hasn't mentioned, reveal it to me by the power of Your holy spirit.

Help me to humble myself and prioritize her heart and needs at this time. Thank You for sending angels of comfort to her bedside at night and for being her sunlight first thing in the morning. I pray sweet memories will flood her mind and that she allows them to make her smile. I pray that You would give her joy unspeakable, even amid the pain. You're a God with a limitless supply of resources. I pray for a supernatural strength over her as she plans any arrangements and as she handles the details of the funeral. I pray against any division that may be trying to rise up in her family's midst right now. I pray that You would cancel the assignment of the enemy that would cause destruction and frustration at such a sorrowful time. I come against everything that would try to cause her any more stress. Heal her heart, Lord. Touch her soul and mind and give her more of You than ever before. In Jesus' name, Amen.

The Breakdown

To be honest, I often wish people's condolences were just as short as this prayer. Over the years, I've learned that some people just don't know what to say when someone loses a family member or loved one. I know that might sound blunt, but I think it's about time somebody says it. As believers, scriptures and the word of God are our heart's joy, but when someone loses a parent, spouse, child, or anyone that they love dearly, oftentimes, we forget that they are human. The whole, "You'll see them again," or "They aren't suffering anymore," sounds good and can be encouraging to some but for many people – they just need to relish in the fact that they just suffered a major loss.

Let them mourn and heal the way God sees fit. Ask God for words of comfort that you can speak. If He doesn't give you any, don't say anything. Just be there. Presence speaks louder than words. Now, those are my personal feelings on the subject. What I really want to focus on is how to respect your friend's healing process after the loss has truly hit her. Here are some practical tips and insight to apply to these situations:

1) ***Don't force what you would want someone to do for you in a similar situation on your friend.*** If your friend states that she wants to be alone, don't you dare tell her she shouldn't be alone right now. Maybe if you were in her shoes, you wouldn't want to be alone,

but people know what they need, even if you think their vulnerability is lying to them. Honor their request.

2) ***Don't force your way into her healing.*** If your friend is finding comfort in her family members, entertainment, or even other friends, the best thing you can do is be supportive when she does reach out to you. I've heard people say some pretty crazy things, and I've even had negative thoughts where I felt left out because I wasn't called on to do something for someone when they lost someone close. It's selfish and has nothing to do with the matter at hand. If you feel like you aren't needed at the moment, pray and love from a distance until you are. There's no need to fight over who is going to support more. Just be supportive and listen out for when God calls you to the front to assist.

3) ***Healing takes time.*** I know people who are still walking through their healing process after suffering a great loss. If the friendship shifts drastically, this isn't the time to bring up things that have been bothering you or hurting you for a long time. As I stated before, be supportive and loving as best you can. If you feel

disconnected from your sister-friend, keep praying and warring. Allow them the time and space to be human; I'll even go as far as to say give them the space to be a little selfish. This may be one of those seasons that they are truly trying to figure out who they are again. Don't disrupt their healing with your pain.

Lastly, it's natural for people to gravitate toward those who may be going through the same valley as them. You may not understand these seasons, but don't connect them to your worth as a friend.

> *You may not understand these seasons, but don't connect them to your worth as a friend.*

Anchor Verse: Psalm 34:18 (TPT)

The Lord is close to all whose hearts are crushed by pain, and he is always ready to restore the repentant one.

Scriptures to meditate on: **Psalm 147:3, Matthew 5:4, 1 Thessalonians 4:17-18**

War 24 - Warring for Her Heart (Bitterness, Resentment, Unforgiveness)

Dear Heavenly Father,

I lift up my sister's heart to You today. She is experiencing some heartache that she's never experienced before. The more she shares with me, the more I realize that she's carrying around some bitterness and resentment. I know these things are breaking her heart, even more than the initial action that caused her such great pain. I'm praying for healing and protection over her heart.

Your word says that You are near to the brokenhearted, and You hear the cries of your children. I'm crying out on her behalf, asking that You would reach down and comfort her. Remind her of Your invaluable presence. If there's anyone she needs to forgive, reveal those names to her and help her to release them to You. Even when she feels like she's still hurt and angry, I pray that You will help her through the process of forgiveness. I pray that You give her perspective about her situation and that she understands that the person who let her down is someone that You love. This isn't easy, Lord. Of course, we both want to lay a different set of hands-on this person, but we know that vengeance is Yours. You will help us to honor You as we deal with feelings of anger, frustration, and resentment. I ask that You help me encourage her to respond in love, even if that means I have to be silent until I know I can speak the right words. If any of these issues are family related, I pray that she understands the importance of taking a step back so that You can heal her heart before she tries to step in and fix the situation on her own. If any childhood wounds have come up, causing her to feel let down by her parents or siblings, Lord, I pray for divine healing over those scars and that when the day comes, You'll use them for Your glory. What the enemy meant for bad, You will turn around and work it out for her good. Thank You for seeing her and for creating her. You know what her destiny looks like, so You will waste nothing that has caused her pain. Thank You that the season is coming where she will once again rejoice. In Jesus' name, Amen.

The Breakdown

Always speak the truth in love – that's the first thing that comes to my mind when I think of this prayer. More importantly, always speak the truth at the right time. I remember sharing my heartache with friends about the absence of my dad. Many times, before I could even finish my story, opinions were shared, and suggestions were given. While people may mean well, the approach to heartbreak, resentment, and bitterness must be handled carefully, especially in friendships.

I remember during my freshman year of college, a friend of mine borrowed twenty dollars from me. I honestly didn't care about the money, and she gave it back. What I didn't like was that our communication had shifted, and I felt like we weren't as close. I finally reached out and asked her what was going on. She admitted that she had stepped back from me because she didn't like the way I had approached her about some of the things going on at work. We were both working part-time at the same job.

Apparently, she had felt like this for some time, long before the money came into play. In a nutshell, she felt like whenever she would share her heart with me, I never knew what to say, even when it came to work-related stuff. I'll raise my hand and say guilty as charged – I didn't know how to talk to my friends, how to communicate that I supported them, and often came off nasty and mean when sharing my heart. At that time (I was nineteen), I had matured some, but there was still major work to be done.

Here she was dealing with her mom and stepfather fighting, feeling like she didn't know who she was because of some personal challenges with a guy she was dating, and dealing with college life and work – and I wasn't being super helpful or supportive in the least bit. I was critical and got straight to the point when giving any advice. I had more of a "get over it" attitude at that age. I had to get over so much of my heartache and pain so quickly that I often felt like others should've been able to do the same.

This story parallels the prayer so well. We never know what is under our friend's pain. If we're not praying for them and asking God to cover their hearts, we risk breaking their hearts as well. Instead of me jumping in and cascading her life with my own experiences, I should've been praying for God to cover her heart. She was struggling to forgive her stepfather for some things he had done to them. She was also dealing with some resentment because her mother often put him before her and her sister. I didn't really know how to pray and war for anyone at that time. While I've always a prayer warrior, my prayers were self-centered at that time. When I did pray for others, it was often with conditions and came from a manipulative place.

> *If we're not praying for them and asking God to cover their hearts, we risk breaking their hearts as well.*

Be the friend that covers your sister's heart daily. Matters of the heart often spill over into every area of our lives. I can't express how grateful I am that now, at thirty-six, I've learned to be the friend who wars and prays immediately. Being in tune with God and flowing with Him has helped me

speak only what He tells me to speak when He tells me to.
You can be mad at what I say all day long, but God doesn't
lie, so as long as I give you His truth, I can be content
knowing that I did my part.

Anchor Verse: Proverbs 4:23 (TPT)

So above all, guard the affections of your heart, for they affect all that you are. Pay attention to the welfare of your innermost being, for from there flows the wellspring of life.

Scriptures to meditate on: **Matthew 5:8, Romans 8:28, Ephesians 4:15**

Here's Your 4th Challenge.

Scan the QR code to watch your challenge on YouTube.

iPhone: Just open your camera and hold it up to the QR code. The link will instantly come up.

Android: You have to download a QR Code reader app.

War 25 - Warring Against Her Blind Spots (She can't see it, but I do...)

Dear Heavenly Father,

Right now, I see some things going on in my friend's world that she isn't able to see. This isn't based on judgment, nor is it based on my own opinion, but I believe that You've revealed something to me about a blind spot that she hasn't recognized. Just like when we drive, and there's a car that's approaching that we can't see, that is exactly how the enemy works. I pray over my sister's blind spots today, the ones where she has a door open to the enemy, and he's wreaking havoc in her life. I pray over the ones that involve her children's life – where she isn't able to see how the enemy has slipped through a crack in her child's life. I pray over the ones that are trying to creep up on her relationship/marriage. Too often, we forget that our fight is not with a person, but with the principalities and rulers of the dark world. You said in Your Word that the enemy roams around like a lion, seeking someone that he can steal, kill, and destroy. I pray right now that You would open my sister's spiritual eyes and ears to recognize the tricks and trades of the enemy. I pray, Lord, that as she raises her children, she understands that not everything is for them. Help her be wise in what she allows her children to listen to, the entertainment they engage in, and the playdates or people she allows them to be around. I pray that she understands the difference between being strict and having a balance that allows You to work in her life and the life of her family members. Help her to cleave more to Your word and Your way of doing things according to Matthew 6:33, versus the opinions of other people around her. I pray against the spirit of counterfeits, and I decree that she will not let one counterfeit enter her life. If there is anyone or anything that wasn't sent by You (a person, business deal, opportunity, etc.), I pray You give her the courage, wisdom, and strength to shut the door promptly.

Help me not to judge her while she's going through this time of trying to implement a strategy to win in this area, but rather to continue to pray and encourage her as You use me to wage war on her behalf. In Jesus' name, Amen.

The Breakdown

I remember when I first started realizing that the things I was watching, listening to, and entertaining were playing a huge role in my life. God actually had me trace back to my childhood and how open my life had been to the enemy's advances very early on. As a woman, when you think about the way a man makes advances toward you and how sometimes, you find yourself feeling uncomfortable in those situations, how do you usually respond? If you're strong and self-aware like me, you're ready to give him a piece of your mind and tell him to kick rocks, especially if you're not interested and you feel he's disrespectfully invaded your space.

The enemy is much like that. He makes advances at us by peering into the areas of our lives that haven't been healed, sealed, or covered by the blood of Christ. Once he knows he can get us to compromise, he will continue to make advances in that area until we're deeply fallen in sin and struggling to get back to a place of wholeness. This is happening regularly in many people's lives. If you're struggling in areas of your life, imagine what your friend is dealing with on her own. Add to that a marriage, children, *and* her career, and you can bet that she's probably overwhelmed. She may not see how some of the seeds that are being planted in her life aren't all coming from God. She may not even understand how those seeds are being planted.

I'll give one example: Most hard-working women these days barely have time for themselves, let alone have time for the families they've built. That's not intentional either. Most women want to do it all, and many can, but not without God's help, wisdom, and grace. With that being said, it's not unusual to find a woman whose child is in front of the television when they come home or who might allow their children to go over to a friend's house for a playdate.

The challenge is, not everyone is raising their children on the same biblical principles as you, and not everyone is aware of the enemy's tricks like you may be. That's why it's important to ask God to reveal to you any areas where there are blind spots that your friend hasn't identified. I would encourage even praying this prayer for yourself because the stronger you are in this area, the more anointing you'll have in this area. Remember, the enemy is sneaky and conniving. He doesn't always creep into these "major" areas that we think about (job loss, divorce, etc.). He does some of his most crafty and cunning work in those crevices and cracks that we've left open.

> *The enemy doesn't always creep into these "major" areas that we think about (job loss, divorce, etc.) — he does some of his most crafty and cunning work in those crevices and cracks that we've left open.*

Some of the areas I have found that the enemy seeps in and wreaks havoc via blind spots are:

1) **Children** – Honestly, children are his favorite because children are so young and innocent; plus, their spirits are still in a sensitive stage. When children are left uncovered (there are layers to this in and of itself) or left indulging in things that can plant seeds of destruction, this can lead to an early spiritual battle that could've been avoided. If you think back on your

own childhood, I'm sure you can recognize some areas where the enemy caused much damage that later had to be overturned in adulthood.

2) **Marriage** – This one isn't what you think. People often think the screaming threats of divorce and infidelity are the highlights of hardships in marriage. While these things are toxic and destructive, I've noticed the enemy often plays his hand much earlier than this. It starts with the small things like being offended that a spouse forgot an important date or event they promised they would attend with you; then leads to you harping on that offense by holding a grudge and not forgiving immediately; which then leads to discussing the offense with other people. All this does is breed contempt and bitterness. Don't water the seeds planted by the enemy.

3) **Counterfeits** – The enemy knows what we want just as much as God does. Now, his knowledge is indeed limited, and he doesn't know all of the details (because He's not God), but he hears us when we discuss our hopes, dreams, and desires. He also hears our prayers. You think he wouldn't try to send a counterfeit to distract you before God sends the real

blessing? Don't Hagar your promise by moving ahead of God's timing.

4) **Selfish Ambitions** – How could I not address this one? Too often, as women of God, we know God is calling us to do great and mighty things, but we tend to lean more toward our selfish desires rather than the desires that we know God placed in our hearts. Selfish ambitions can ultimately be a trap of the enemy. I mean, what's wrong with giving back and starting a non-profit that may change the world, right? Let me ask you this: would you rather pursue a 'good idea' or a 'God idea'? God is not obligated to back up a good idea. If it comes out of our own desires, we need to check and make sure we aren't settling for the good when God has so much more for us.

These can be huge blind spots for us because the enemy doesn't come with a huge red pitchfork and horns. He comes dressed up in a nice suit, smelling good and looking like everything we ever dreamed of. Remember, the enemy is much more subtle and conniving. The same way God's voice is often in the whisper is similar to the enemy being in the subtle things. Only his small things often lead to a big, loud crash.

Anchor Verse: 1 Peter 5:8 (TPT)

Be well balanced and always alert, because your enemy, the devil, roams around incessantly, like a roaring lion looking for its prey to devour.

Scriptures to meditate on: **Ephesians 6:11-17, John 10:10, 2 Corinthians 11:14**

War 26 - Warring for Her Job/Career/Business

Dear Heavenly Father,

My friend has had a long and fruitful career. I pray that as she continues to serve at this place You've assigned to her, that she will continue to flourish and grow in her skillset. I also pray that You would reveal to her why You've placed her there if she doesn't already know. Show her the people who are assigned to her at her place of work, so that she can be a light and fulfill her assignment.

I pray that she humbles herself and realizes that You didn't just place her there to work for them but to also work for You. Reveal to her any areas of weakness so that she can submit them to You. Help her understand how this job can help her to grow in those areas. As she performs her work duties, help her to operate in a spirit of excellence. I pray against any work conflict and ask that You would give her insight into any spiritual battles that have erected. I pray for her boss and colleagues and ask that You help them all find balance as they work together. I decree that they will respect and honor her. I pray that she will be confident in her contributions to the company and what she has to offer. Help her trust You and help her believe that what You've placed inside of her is needed in this hour. Thank You for giving her vision to see herself beyond this moment so that when You shift her via a promotion, or even into a leap of faith in another direction, she can see that what she's learned at this job will help her. Give her the wisdom and strength to pass every test that will come her way at her job. Show her how to navigate this season with wisdom and how to use her weapons wisely. Remind her daily that she doesn't wrestle against flesh and blood, but against rulers of the dark world, principalities, and the prince of the air. Help her walk in every day and pray over her place of work before everyone arrives. Remind her of the spiritual authority that she has. Help her to see that she may be the only Jesus that someone encounters. In Jesus' name, Amen.

The Breakdown

We spend much of our time at work. Most of us spend at least forty hours a week at our place of work. No matter how much we love what we do, it doesn't take away the idea that we will face incidents and go through challenges. There are times when I found myself complaining about a situation at work, forgetting that I had authority over the atmosphere. This isn't something to brush off or to take lightly. Our authority is how we navigate those seasons of spiritual warfare. If we can just grasp this one concept – that all of our battles are spiritual – I think we would be better equipped to wage war with the enemy instead of people. Now, this doesn't mean that conversations won't take place to help bring resolution to the conflict, but it does mean that as believers, we have something the world doesn't have – authority in Christ.

Use your authority and stop letting the enemy punk you out of your place of work, your marriage, and your calling. So many of us quote scripture but don't take the time to apply it when we're in the thick of the battle. I can't stress this enough – use your authority. Praying for your sister in this way will help cover her in an area that she may be growing in. Not everyone understands the spiritual realm, and God may be advancing you in that area first because He knows you will take heed and listen. In another season, she may be stronger in that area than you and will be able to help you wage war when you don't realize you're up against a new devil.

With that knowledge, when we walk into our place of work, there should be something different about us. People should be able to sense that we aren't like them – in a refreshing way. Whether it's the joy in our hearts or our way of talking or *not* talking, something should pique their interest to ask us about the "Who" and "why" of our lives. This doesn't mean mistakes won't be made, but it does mean

> *Nothing we do for the Kingdom or for Christ will be without pressure.*

that the scent of Christ will enter these atmospheres, and we should be ready to respond when people ask. Having this understanding will help you take prayer into your workplace and to be an example. If you feel like that's a weight, it is. Nothing we do for the Kingdom or for Christ will be without pressure.

It's growing you and stretching your faith in areas where you may not have been using them. Because of that, leaving the job won't change the test you have to pass. It'll just be a new location and a new set of people, but the devil will still be there. God doesn't just send you somewhere blindly, and He doesn't waste anything. If you're a praying woman, then God opened the door for you to be at that job. Every season we're in is preparing us for the next season. Get all the "on-the-job" training you can get. I had to start looking at these moments as God allowing me to receive a paycheck while being in seminary at the same time. I was getting the lessons and blessings. You will have to see it the same way. You also have to acknowledge that God has placed something inside of you to handle what you're dealing with at work and to even bring value to your place of work.

When I was a substitute teacher in Philadelphia, I remember experiencing a level of spiritual warfare that I had never encountered. Children tend to carry spirits because they are more susceptible to the enemy's tactics. Just like babies have weaker immune systems than adults, children have weaker spiritual immunity, and if a parent hasn't been covering and protecting their child from seeds of darkness being planted into their children's lives, then their susceptibility to the illnesses of the enemy is higher.

By week two, I was carrying oil to work, covering the seats and the classroom door before the children got there. I remember God telling me to walk around the classroom and pray, which he confirmed that I was doing the right thing through a spiritual mentor of mine. I believe God used that as a training ground so that I would be prepared to handle where he was taking me next, which was Hollywood. If I couldn't handle the demons in a classroom, how could I handle the ones in Hollywood?

Commercial Break: Didn't I tell ya'll that I don't hold no punches? Either we're gonna be the church or we're not. Real recognizes real and it's about time we continue to expose the enemy and his schemes. Simply put: Know your enemy. Know your war. Use your weapons. Win the war.

> *Simply put: Know your enemy. Know your war. Use your weapons. Win the war.*

Anchor Verse: Ecclesiastes 9:10 (NKJV)

Whatever your hand finds to do, do it with your might; for there is no work or device or knowledge or wisdom in the grave where you are going.

Scriptures to meditate on: **Proverbs 16:3, Isaiah 48:17, Ecclesiastes 11:6**

War 27 - Warring for Her Dreams

Dear Heavenly Father,

My friend has been praying about these dreams in her heart for a long time. She's been on a unique journey, and You've placed an anointing on her life for this God-sized dream. I pray that You would give her the patience to walk through every season and understand its importance to her dream. Give her the strength and fortitude not to give up. You placed this dream in her heart because Your plan for her life is bigger than what she realizes.

Help her to continue to write the vision and make it plain. Help her to see beyond this moment, but only give her what she can handle right now. Help me to be supportive by only speaking life over her dream. If I'm not sure what to say, help me keep my mouth shut except to pray. Give me words of encouragement that will help my sister. Lead me to scriptures to send her while she's going through the journey. Any opportunities that arise, I pray a fasting spirit over her, so that she knows what to say, "yes" to and what to say "no" to. Help her realize that not every door is for her. I pray that she has a safe space to discuss her dreams with her mate/spouse. I pray that he honors her dreams and even pushes her to go after them. I pray that she will know how to trust You while waiting for each season of her dream to manifest. Help her understand that there isn't a straight path to her dreams, but that You are leading her along the path that's best for her. As she draws inspiration from those who've gone before her in this arena, help her not to compare her journey with others, but to embrace her story. I pray for the resources, tools, mentors, and insight she needs to pursue her dream and to embrace the fullness of it. If she's pursuing a dream that You didn't place in her heart, I pray that You redirect her right now. Lead her to the dream You know will bring her happiness and fulfillment. I pray that she can identify the dream that's tied to purpose and destiny and not just the one that points to wealth and great networking. I pray that if she has to be redirected, that You give her the strength to lay down her plan and to pick up Yours. You know us better than we know ourselves – so help her to see that You know what she needs to bring fulfillment and purpose to her life and the lives of those You've assigned to her name. In Jesus' name, Amen.

The Breakdown

Dreams are beautiful. Dreams are potential. Dreams, done God's way, can bring you into a lifetime of overflow and blessings. Dreams are also scary, hard, and overwhelming. If I told you how many times I wanted to give up on my dreams, you would probably inquire, "Well, why didn't you?". What makes going after dreams so beautiful is that there's a deep knowing in your spirit that you can't ignore. It's one thing to have an idea or a dream that you think is something you want to pursue. It's another thing to have a dream that *you* were called to pursue. Dreams are God's way of placing an imprint of purpose in our hearts to lead us along the path that will bring Him glory and fulfill our earthly assignment. Simple as that. But the road to those dreams being fulfilled is tough, and only the strong, resilient, and faithful survive.

> *Dreams are God's way of placing an imprint of purpose in our hearts to lead us along the path that will bring Him glory and fulfill our earthly assignment.*

What you don't want or need while pursuing a dream is a narcissistic, negative, and belittling individual around telling you how that dream is impossible. You want and need praying friends who understand that even if they don't see how you're going to do something, they can help pray for the wisdom for you to get that thing done. You need "riders" who may not currently have big things going on but will root for you because they want you to do great. Going after what God placed in your heart is hard enough with your own doubts and unbelief that will arise. The people surrounding you (close to you) should be able to either handle what you're carrying, or they need to step aside and pray for new friends to arise who can help you carry your dream.

This is why whenever God is leading you into a new season, he will often set you apart so that it's just you and Him. Do you know why most dreams don't come to pass for people or why so many people find themselves failing time and time again? The process to get from seed to dream manifested requires a lot of time alone. It requires separation and sacrifice on another level.

> *The process to get from seed to dream manifested requires a lot of time alone. It requires separation and sacrifice on another level.*

Too many people are concerned about everyone being on board with their dreams that they can't even hear what God is saying. Nothing hurts more than seeing someone with the resources, finances, and even vision to birth their dream into existence, but because they don't have the support system in place, they don't take the first step toward that dream. Be the woman that's rooting for your friends' God-given dream even when she doesn't fully believe in herself. Pray her into faith.

When I first started out on the journey to become a writer, I had my own fears and concerns. It was hard for me to see beyond my dream of being a Pediatrician because I wanted safety. I took my first leap of faith at twenty-seven. I moved to Atlanta, and that's where so much of my writing dream was fed. I may have told a few people, but I left without sharing it with many people. I knew that if I didn't just go, I would regret it and be questioning it forever. Since then, I've taken numerous leaps of faith and found myself in great rooms and walking through some pretty big doors.

I have a great friend that has always prayed over me and rooted for me, even though we have completely different lifestyles. Not once has she questioned whether or not I know what I'm doing or if I'm hearing from God. She trusts what God has placed in my heart and has supported me – even with financial blessings – to help me get closer to where I believe God is calling me. Even when I would find myself failing, she never said, "Why don't you just get a regular job and call it quits?" She's there when I need her and prays when I need it. That's the type of friend you need in your corner. You need someone that's going to wage war for your blessings while you're pursuing them.

Anchor Verse: Psalm 20:4 (TPT)

May God give you every desire of your heart and carry out your every plan as you go to battle.

Scriptures to meditate on: **Hebrews 11:1, 2 Chronicles 15:7, Ecclesiastes 5:3**

War 28 - Warring for Her Home & Community (Proverbs 31 Woman)

Dear Heavenly Father,

I am praying the prayer of Proverbs 31 over my friend. I pray that not only does she continue to work according to what You gave her, but that she will be able to enjoy the works of her hand. I pray that her family will give her the space to rest and be. Thank You for a husband that sees her the way You do. I pray that he honors and covers her the way she honors and covers him. I pray that he will rise up and call her blessed. I pray that she is valued in her home and in her community. I pray against the enemy's tactics to bring unnecessary guilt over her life. I thank You that those who love her would be mouthpieces that prophesy over her life. I pray that they would continue to appreciate the radiance of who she is and all that she carries. Thank You that they will always see her in the image and likeness of God. As she continues to feed those around her, both spiritually and physically, I pray that she will be fed, also. I pray she takes time to sit at your feet and allow You to feed her spirit, knowing that no matter what, what she needs most will always come from You first. I pray that she will continue to wrap herself in your strength and might. Thank You that everything she touches, from her home to her community, to her business, will flourish because she values excellence. Thank You that her husband's heart trusts in her. Thank You that whenever her husband and children speak of her, they do so in loving terms and by extolling her. I pray that she will always walk in the bold power and glorious majesty that You've rested on her. When she's tempted to cave in, I pray that she remembers You anointed her to walk in this manner, and she can handle whatever comes her way. Help them all keep You first so that they understand how to see each other properly. I pray she receives all the credit due to her name. In Jesus' name, Amen.

The Breakdown

Too often, women pour from an empty cup. They pour from a place of pain, tiredness, and frustration. Nothing hurts more than feeling like you're giving everyone around you your all, but you can't even get someone to bring you a glass of water when you're thirsty. This prayer is about you praying for those she pours into daily. This could be her spouse, children, family, her job – everyone, including you. Pray that those she loves and pours into will give her the flowers she deserves while she's alive. We hear this so often – that people wish they had given someone they really loved and appreciated their flowers while they were alive.

Pray that she not only continues to be a Proverbs 31 woman, but that her children will truly rise up and call her blessed. Pray that her parents and those she helps care for will honor, support, and love her. Pray that they reverence her. This means you'll need to pray against the spirit of selfishness and dishonor that's hovering in her space. She might feel it and even speak on it, but she needs you to war for it. Sometimes, her silent cries to God will be a simple, "God, help me," while you – the warring friend – will be in the corner, grabbing the enemy by his ugly head and telling him to release the mind of your friend's children and husband so they can see her clearly.

Women aren't just helpmates – they are heroes. This isn't about placing her on a pedestal, but it is about acknowledging God in her. Walking in purpose requires extreme focus and women are often criticized for their lack of focus before they're celebrated for their contributions. Yes, she should be focused on her family, but her needs shouldn't go dismissed. She wants to live out her purpose just as much as she pours into the family around her, to make sure they have the means to live out theirs.

> *She wants to live out her purpose just as much as she pours into the family around her, to make sure they have the means to live out theirs.*

Pray for seasons of grace and understanding from her mate (potential mate as well). Bind the spirits of neglect and disrespect on her behalf. I say this respectfully, but she will probably always put her needs last. Pray that God will stretch the capacity of those around her. If they're assigned to her life, then they have what it takes to support her in every season. It may not be perfect, and they may even feel a bit slighted, but relationships are about service and sacrifice. There shouldn't only be one person doing all of that.

Anchor verse: Proverbs 31:31 (TPT)

So, go ahead and give her the credit that is due, for she has become a radiant woman, and all her loving works of righteousness deserve to be admired at the gateways of every city!

Scriptures to meditate on: **Proverbs 31 (whole chapter)**

War 29 - Warring for Her Finances (Stewardship & Boundaries)

Dear Heavenly Father,

I lift up my sister's finances to You this day. I ask that You touch her finances and all increase that is on its way to her. According to Your word, I decree that she will be a faithful tither and trust You with her finances. As she seeks first the kingdom of God, I pray that You would add all other things unto her. I pray that she would have full confidence that every seed she's ever sown will yield a harvest at the correct time. I pray that You would give her wisdom and insight into how to manage and steward her finances well. Her current provision is based on her current assignment. Help her to understand that You won't give her more than she can handle at any given time. As she continues to work and puts her hand to the plow, help her trust that You will take the 90% she has remaining and make it stretch. I thank You that the devourer can't destroy what she has planted and that You are rebuking him for her sake. I pray that she would be wise in her saving and spending. Any fruitless thing that she is doing, help her stop immediately. Thank You that she and her mate will have wise conversations surrounding their money. I pray against the spirit of fear regarding the risk, You've told them to take and that they would trust You for the outcome. I pray over her business finances, their real estate finances, and any other field that you lead them to tend. I pray for favor with banks and investors. I pray the spirit of ownership over her and her family, decreeing that she will be blessed more and more, her and her children. Lastly, I pray that we would both use wisdom in borrowing and lending money to each other. Help us to understand the concept of deposits and withdrawals and to keep a healthy balance in our friendship as it pertains to finances, even if that means setting up a boundary of not loaning money to one another. Give us wisdom on the timing that we should just sow a blessing into one another's lives. I pray she manages her money well and that her 'no' be 'no' and her 'yes' be 'yes'. In Jesus' name, Amen.

The Breakdown

Finances are a tough conversation to have in any relationship. The challenge with having the conversation in a friendship is that usually, it's someone asking to borrow money or someone asking for their money to be returned. Most friends don't know how to balance this out, causing many good friendships to end in despair. I'm going to share a few things below to give you some insight and wisdom on finances and friendships:

1) Except for the four times in my life when I was in dire need, I don't borrow money from friends. One of those times was someone offering it to me as a loan, and the other times were extreme circumstances. One of the other times, I could barely pay the person back, and my mom had to step in and pay it. With that being said, do not fall victim to the mindset that because your friend has it, you should have it. I do

believe that God will orchestrate our friends to sow into our lives and bless us when we're in need. He uses people to bless us, but don't place that burden of responsibility on your friends. I also think we have to be careful gauging people's financial situations based on what they have or what they have acquired. Just because you have a successful friend who earns good money, this doesn't give you the right to analyze her checkbook and do the guesswork of how much she can help you. This is a sneaky way of seeking help. When I was in my early twenties, my perception of someone's situation often led me to believe that they weren't struggling themselves.

2) Clear boundaries should be put in place the first-time money comes up in a friendship. What are your boundaries, and what are hers? Is she willing to be a blessing without expecting the money in return, or is she clearly stating that she wants her money back? Whatever those boundaries are, honor them. Don't be the friend that burns a bridge. Being honest about your financial situation also helps. If you can't pay it back, make it clear so that she understands.

3) If you're naturally a giver, then give as God leads. Don't give and then get frustrated that the person you sowed into isn't responding to you the way you feel they should. I remember a time when I was able to be a blessing financially to people, that I would often feel let down when they weren't calling and checking on me every day, or we didn't get to hang out as often. It was like I believed their friendship obligation to me should've increased just because I had helped them. So, while I wasn't asking for the money back, I was asking for something in return. Some would say I was trying to buy the friendship. One has nothing to do with the other, so don't let finances put unnecessary pressure on your friendships.

4) Someone else's urgency is not your emergency. In other words, just because someone mismanaged their funds, this doesn't mean you owe them anything. So often, people are frustrated about their own financial situation, and then they take that frustration out on

Just because you have a successful friend who earns good money, this doesn't give you the right to analyze her checkbook and do the guesswork of how much she can help you.

others. There's a big difference between helping in a time of need and enabling. Don't end up rescuing someone who should be depending on God for their needs. Again, whenever you're going to be involved in somebody else's miracle, God will lead you, and there will be peace. If there isn't any peace, don't do it.

I've seen far too many friendships and family relationships become strained due to this. It's not about someone being selfish, either. Think about the chapter on valuing your friend over supporting her. When you value someone, you value them through and through. Every area of their lives should be valued by you, even if you don't share those same exact values on that subject. Financial matters are no different. I've had great friends throughout the years sow into my life. I've traveled the road of a very unique dream as a writer, and God has blessed me with friends who sowed into my life throughout every season. I couldn't be any more grateful. I also know that this isn't the average person's narrative. A lot of people believe in me, and they know that once God sends that breakthrough, I'll not only bless those around me, but I'll reach back and sow into the lives of those who've helped me.

Anchor Verse: Proverbs 26:18-19 (TPT)

The one who is caught lying to his friend and says, "I didn't mean it, I was only joking," can be compared to a madman randomly shooting off deadly weapons.

Scriptures to meditate on: **Deuteronomy 23:19-20, Luke 6:38, Psalm 15:5**

War 30 - Warring for Her Blessings

Dear Heavenly Father,

I'm tired of my friend dealing with these delays and hindrances that are holding up her blessings. We know that You do all things well and that You have set the timing for our blessings to be released into our lives. You also know what and who we need and where we need to be to receive those blessings. However, I feel in my spirit that the enemy is waging war against her and that he is the reason and cause for the delay. I believe the resistance that she has been feeling as she continues to stand in faith and obedience is a direct result of spiritual warfare. Father, I pray that she will continue to contend for what

You've placed in her heart. I pray that You would give her the
desires of her heart – give her those things that will please
and bring glory to You. Thank You for giving her the
confidence to believe in these things and to know that You're
a God who wants to see your children living in the fullness of
Your promises. I command the enemy to release everything
that belongs to her. I wage war against hell and reach into hell
with her to take hold of all the things that have her name on
it. Her peace, her joy, her restoration, her strength –
everything that he thought he could take from her, I
command him to release it and give it back right now. Every
spirit of python that has entered the different areas of her life,
I command that spirit of python to go back to the pits of hell
where it belongs. I refuse to see her lose. Your word says that
we have a never-ending victory in Christ Jesus. Victory
belongs to Jesus. You already defeated the enemy at the cross
and then defeated him again when You rose from the dead.
Father, all the things that she thinks are dead in her life, I ask
that You breathe life into them according to Your perfect
will. I pray that dry bones would arise and that whatever
blessings You want her to have in this season, that there
would be no delay. Lastly, if there is anything that she's
holding onto that can't go into this new season with her, I

pray that You give her the strength to release it and let it go. We thank You for all the spoils that she will collect after this war is over. In Jesus' name, Amen.

The Breakdown

Warring for your sister's blessings is about more than praying that she'll be blessed and receive the things she's praying for. Far too often, we think friendship is cute. We think it's "let's get together and have a slumber party like when we were younger" cute. The reality is friendships can get just as dirty as a marriage. You will have seasons where you have to fight the enemy with your friend, and the battle will rarely leave you with your lace front in place or your eyelashes still on. This thing could turn bloody when you both rise up to fight the enemy that tries to disrupt God's plans for both of your lives.

> *You will have seasons where you have to fight the enemy with your friend, and the battle will rarely leave you with your lace front in place or your eyelashes still on.*

Friendships aren't for the faint of heart because real friendships will go through unprecedented, ugly times. There will be times where your friend may be in a state of mind that you never thought you would see her in. I want the kind of friends that I don't have to ask to pray for me. Simply put, if I call you and tell you something is going on, save the questions for after we pray. That's not me being mean, either. That's the kind of friend that I am and the kind of friend that I desire.

Don't just pray for surface level blessings either. A relationship with Christ is rooted in so much more. It's rooted in The Gospel's very desire to see us set free from anything that could be holding us back. This could mean getting down and dirty in your prayer closet and often having to reveal in love what God tells you to share with her. She may be believing God for her next promotion, but God told you to pray that she can receive correction from her current boss before she receives a promotion. In that case, you pray that God will continue to cover her and that she hears clearly what she needs to do to prepare.

I remember sharing my pain of some of my financial struggles with a friend of mine in 2017. I had no idea how I was going to pay my car insurance, and I was on the verge of being dropped from the insurance company. Listen, we all have financial struggles and challenges. That's life, but I know that the enemy has waged war against my finances ever since I was young. I could feel the spirit of poverty resting on my family's bloodline, and I knew it was about more than "missing a few" bills. Once I understood that I was experiencing heavy bouts of spiritual warfare throughout my life, I started to grasp why he would hit me hard in my finances (this doesn't include any season where I didn't steward well).

So, back to the story. This was during the time my mother had tongue cancer for the second time. I was trying to navigate a part-time job while being her support system – not to mention I was trying to build a new stream of income. To reach out to my friend (it was an inbox message) and receive a response that inquired about what insurance company I was with and why I needed to switch was a huge blow to my heart. Not because that may not be an option for later, but because right now, switching wouldn't do anything because I would still need money to switch. All I was doing was asking for her prayers, which I included in the message. By the way, this doesn't take anything away from her being a great friend.

Warring for your friend's blessings is knowing when a cry for help needs to be turned into a prayer request. It's pausing before responding and allowing the Holy Spirit to provide insight and understanding before saying something that could make your friend feel like she shouldn't have ended up in the situation in the first place. The blessings I'm speaking of aren't just tangible, either. This is about warring for the mental, emotional, physical, and social blessings your friend desires and is believing God for. War is real. Let's show up to the war ready to win.

Anchor Verse: 1 Chronicles 12:1-2 (NKJV)

Now these were the men who came to David at Ziklag while he was still a fugitive from Saul the son of Kish; and they were among the mighty men, helpers in the war, armed with bows, using both the right hand and the left in hurling stones and shooting arrows with the bow. They were of Benjamin, Saul's brethren.

Scriptures to meditate on: **1 Chronicles 12:8, 2 Chronicles 20:25, 1 Samuel 17:47**

Here's Your 5th and FINAL Challenge.

Scan the QR code to watch your challenge on YouTube.

iPhone: Just open your camera and hold it up to the QR code. The link will instantly come up.

Android: You have to download a QR Code reader app.

Conclusion

B y now, I pray that you realize these prayers aren't just for wives, mothers, or women who are entrepreneurs. These prayers are meant to be proactive so that even before these moments come, you can war on your sister friend's behalf, especially as she believes God for wholeness in these very areas. No matter what, take these prayers, and whatever way you need to readjust the words to fit your situation, do so.

And while women may find this book to be a hidden gem now discovered, I wrote this book for girls of all ages. With society constantly putting girls and women against each other, a tool like this is invaluable, especially in the body of Christ. It's in the younger years of our lives where we long for great friendships the most. I believe this book will touch the hearts of young girls and women for two reasons:

1) We all long for connection, and…

2) Because we all have the same enemy – Satan. The battle for each person may be different, but the enemy is indeed the same.

The enemy could care less about your age. If he can get you to walk in jealousy and fear, he will. If he can keep you bound to feelings of unworthiness because of neglect and misunderstandings, he will. He fights against us from the moment we're born, so why should we wait until we're in "the" situation to wage war against him? He doesn't play fair, so neither should we. War for your girls – from the college zone to the career zone and watch God move mightily on your behalf.

> *The devil fights against us from the moment we're born, so why should we wait until we're in "the" situation to wage war against him? He doesn't play fair, so neither should we.*

Reason, Season & Lifetime

If there's one thing I've learned throughout life, it's the importance of quality over quantity. With that being said, God's design for friendships is often laid out in the concept: *reason, season, or lifetime.* We're always connecting with people. Even when I taught for a year in South Korea, I connected with many people who helped guide me through that season. With the language barriers and the other disconnects we may have had, there was one thing I knew for certain – they had been handpicked by God to help see me through. It's amazing how an app can build a whole friendship (smile).

Never feel defeated when you end up no longer connecting with someone like you used to. Remember when I stated how concerned I am when someone has a bunch of friends? It's because the reality is, someone is probably holding on too long. Don't fill your voids with people. Don't try to build up your contact list so you can keep yourself preoccupied and neglect working on your issues. I did it for too long, and after the phone stopped ringing, those issues were still there. I know there has been much shared on the topic of reason, season, or a lifetime, but I'd like to take it a step further and provide the following insight as we close this thing out.

Those who you connect with for a reason will always play a significant role in your life for a moment. Those you connect with for a season will always play a valuable role in your life for a season. Those you're blessed to connect with for a lifetime will play an eternal role throughout your life. That lifetime number is few. In fact, there's only room for a few. I believe God does this because the more you grow and evolve in Him, there are only a few people assigned to you (which will include your spouse), who can handle the full weight of who you are. Let God curate those lifetime friendships. Haven't we learned by now? His craftsmanship is unbeatable.

Bonus Prayer - Warring for Her Protection

Dear Heavenly Father,

I decree protection over my sister according to Your Word in Psalm 91. I declare that despite any tactics of the enemy, she will go to the grave at a ripe old age according to Job 5:26. Father, I decree a hedge of protection around her, from the crown of her head to the soles of her feet. I dispatch angels on her behalf to show up when she's up against trouble, harm, or danger. I pray supernatural protection around her, the same way You supernaturally protected the Hebrew boys that ended up in the fiery furnace. I decree sound wisdom over her life as it pertains to her travels and daily activities. I pray that she would allow You to lead her every footstep. If You tell her not to go someplace, I pray she obeys that prompting in her spirit. I pray she would listen when she is somewhere, and there's a prompting to leave. You see the end from the beginning, and You know all things – so I thank You right now that she will always trust You over any man or woman. I pray that she will not be blinded by the enemy's schemes – that she will always be able to see into someone's character, their motives, and their intentions. I pray that she would pray about every connection, every assignment, every task – so that she can follow Your lead and stay safe. I pray right now that she will not taste death early – that no weapon formed against her will prosper and that she will look beyond the surface, to see into the spirit. You will never lead her astray, so if You say 'no,' let it be so. I pray that she has ears to hear the wisdom of those around her, who may see and be aware of something that she's not. I pray that she won't go anywhere that Your hand hasn't led her – this goes for relationships, friendships, gatherings, events, and homes. I pray that she only connects with those movements and ideas that You've assigned to her and not those she's been pressured to be a part of. I pray for protection over her life, her possessions, and her peace. Lord, grant her the serenity to yield to Your will even if it's not the way she would've chosen. In Jesus' name, Amen.

The Breakdown

On July 11th, 2020, I was on my way to a hair appointment – a six in the morning hair appointment, ladies. Don't judge me. While driving down the street, I saw a young lady with her thumb sticking out, like a hitchhiker, but I kept going. It was about 5:30 in the morning, and I'm always about safety first. But then I heard a sound which sounded a lot like crying. I looked in my rearview mirror and tried to make out what was going on, but only saw her – a young, white female with long-hair. She had a backpack on with a yellow shirt and shorts. She didn't look like she could harm me, but I was not playing about this hair appointment. I know, I know. Shallow, right?

But if you know anything about growing up in Philadelphia, then you know that giving the side-eye before actually lending a helping hand is normal. In fact, it's encouraged. After about a minute, while I was sitting at the stop sign, I finally put my car in reverse and backed up down the street. Not only did I notice immediate relief on her face, but I could read the stress all over her tear-stained face – and I could hear it in her voice. The details:

She walked all the way from Fox Chase to where I was in East Oak Lane. For my city people that know the distance, this girl was clearly desperate to get to her destination. That's over an hour of walking. She explained that she had gone to a party with her friends and she felt uncomfortable and wanted to leave. Apparently, she felt so uncomfortable that she refused to wait for them and decided to walk. She asked me how to get to the subway that would take her back to her college campus. I told her that she was only a few blocks away and needed to walk straight down 11th Street, and she would run right into it. That was all she wanted. Direction. I asked her if she needed me to call the police, and she said 'no,' so I gave her a smile, then turned around and headed to my destination.

Back at the same stop sign, I couldn't stop thinking about what I would want someone to do if that was my little sister. The Holy Spirit prompted me to turn back around and take her to the train station. When I pulled up alongside her, she started crying again and said that she would be fine. I put on my best Momma voice and told her to get in the car. I didn't feel safe letting a young lady who was already frantic walk to the train station at five-something in the morning. Again, relief washed over her face. While riding to the station, we talked. I learned that she was a freshman in college and had gone to a party with some friends, and whatever happened there didn't make her feel comfortable.

I asked her why she didn't get an Uber home, and she said she didn't want to wait there. That left a horrible feeling in the pit of my stomach. What on earth had happened with these so-called "friends" that she wouldn't even wait for an Uber? Instead of speculating, I began to minister to her spirit and told her a little of my own story. I had walked alone throughout my college years plenty of times because I just wouldn't follow the crowd. When we pulled up to the train station, I prayed over her and encouraged her to always "leave" any space or place where she doesn't feel safe – even if you have to leave alone.

That's what this prayer is about. So many of our girls end up in crazy situations because they're concerned about what people will think if they "don't take the drink" or "don't go to the bedroom with that guy". To this day, I have no idea what she was running from, but what I do know is that I let her know how proud of her I was. Our daughters are facing enough challenges and struggles without having to worry about their lives being in danger because they are at the wrong place, at the wrong time. This prayer is also about covering our daughters, who won't always be in our eyesight. Whenever I think about the countless young ladies who have lost their lives for being connected to the wrong guy, or the wrong people, it pains me to think the enemy wants our girls so bad that he will send destruction in any way that he can.

But we have the upper hand. We can war for our girls without hesitation by praying the word and decreeing Psalm 91 over their lives daily. When you feel that prompting in your spirit to pray for someone, you don't need to know why – just begin to pray this prayer and recite Psalm 91, incorporating their name into the prayer. Trust me. This prayer has dispatched angels on my behalf countless times, and I know God will do the same for you and that friend you're warring for.

Anchor Verse: Psalm 91:9-11 (TPT)

When we live our lives within the shadow of God Most High, our secret hiding place, we will always be shielded from harm. How then could evil prevail against us or disease infect us?

God sends angels with special orders to protect you wherever you go, defending you from all harm.

Scripture to meditate on: **Job 5:26, Psalm 91 (whole chapter)**

About Mya K. Douglas

Born and raised in North Philadelphia, Mya Kay is an author, educator, and speaker. With a passion to help women and teen girls heal from their trauma, Mya K. Douglas, professionally known as Mya Kay, launched Girls Anthem in the fall of 2019 with one goal – to make God proud. Girls Anthem is a multi-faceted movement designed to equip women and teen girls with the tools they need to pursue destiny without compromising their values or their stories. *Warring for My Girls* is the first book released under the Girls Anthem umbrella and aims to bring healing to friendships, from the college zone to the career zone. She is the creator and host of "The Girl Files", a podcast that propels women and girls into healing, using spoken word, The Gospel, and down-to-earth storytelling. Earlier in her career, she penned a total of twelve books, including, *The Clover Chronicles: Battling*

Brelyn and *Before Empire: Raising Bryshere "Yazz the Greatest" Gray*. You can learn more about her at www.writermya.com and www.girlsanthem.biz. Follow her on social media @writermya.

www.ingramcontent.com/pod-product-compliance
Lightning Source LLC
LaVergne TN
LVHW051231080426
835513LV00016B/1530